TOOTHBRUSH YOGA

Tiny Habits, Transformative Results

ROB HALES

Copyright Information

Toothbrush Yoga: Tiny Habits, Transformational Results

© Copyright 2023 by Rob Hales

All rights reserved. No part of this publication may be reproduced, distributed, or transmitted in any form or by any means, including photocopying, recording, or other electronic or mechanical methods, without the prior written permission of the publisher, except in the case of brief quotations embodied in critical reviews and certain other non-commercial uses permitted by copyright law. For permission requests, please contact the author directly.

By: Rob Hales

Disclaimer

This book is for informational purposes only. The content provided herein is based on the author's personal experiences and research. It is not intended to be a substitute for professional medical advice, diagnosis, or treatment. Always seek the advice of your physician or other qualified health provider with any questions you may have regarding a medical condition. Never disregard professional medical advice or delay in seeking it because of something you have read in this book.

The author and publisher specifically disclaim all responsibility for any liability, loss, or risk, personal or otherwise, which is incurred as a consequence, directly or indirectly, of the use and application of any of the contents of this book.

Please note the information contained within this document is for educational and entertainment purposes only. All effort has been executed to present accurate, up-to-date, reliable, and complete information. No warranties of any kind are declared or implied.

You acknowledge that the author is not engaged in the rendering of legal, financial, medical, or professional advice. The content within this book has been derived from various sources.

The author and publisher of this book cannot be held responsible for any injuries sustained as a result of attempting the yoga poses within, nor can they be held responsible for any newfound obsession with yoga or the wearing of any fluorescent Lycra clothing as a result of reading this book.

By reading this document, you agree that under no circumstances is the author responsible for any losses, direct or indirect, that are incurred because of the use of the information contained within this document, including, but not limited to, errors, omissions, or inaccuracies.

Trademark Information

All terms mentioned in this book that are known to be trademarks or service marks have been appropriately capitalised. The author and the publisher cannot attest to the accuracy of this information. Use of a term in this book should not be regarded as affecting the validity of any trademark or service mark.

Contents

Preface — 5

Introducing Toothbrush Yoga — Tiny Habits, Transformational Results — 7
   Bite-Sized Yoga — Less than 2 Minutes — 8
   Am I Too Old? — 8
   What Does Yoga Do for You? — It's Way More Than Just Stretching — 9

My Path to Becoming a Toothbrush Yogi — 11

Chapter 1: The Triad of Transformation: Outcomes, Identity, and Goals — 21
   Outcomes: Defining Your Destination — 21
   Identity/Beliefs: Shaping Your Self-Perception — 22
   Goals: Milestones of Progress — 24

Chapter 2: The Hidden Forces — Decoding the Mechanisms of Habits — 27
   Cracking the Habit Code — Unleashing the Power of Daily Habits — 28

Chapter 3: Hijacking the Habit Flow — 33
   Beyond Routines: How Habit Stacking Amplifies the Power of Small — 35
   Let's Work Through a Toothbrush Yoga Example — Brushing your Teeth — 36

Chapter 4: My Toothbrush Yoga Framework — Morning Ritual — 39

Chapter 5: Toothbrush Yoga at Work/Study — 47

Chapter 6: Toothbrush Yoga in Everyday Tasks — 49

Chapter 7: Toothbrush Yoga in Evening Rituals — 53

Chapter 8: Your Toothbrush Yoga Framework — 57
   STEP 1 — Setting Your Course — Your Desired Outcomes — 59
   STEP 2 — Navigating Your Path — Identity and Beliefs — 61
   STEP 3 — Fuelling the Journey — Your Toothbrush Yoga Intentions — 62
   STEP 4 — Creating your Personalised Morning Ritual — 65
   STEP 5 — The Power of Priority — Ranking Your Morning Habits — 66
   STEP 6 — Strike a Pose — 68

STEP 7 — Harnessing the Power of Association 70

STEP 8 — Reaping the Rewards 73

STEP 9 — Continuing the Flow — Evening Ritual and Beyond 75

STEP 10 — Plotting and Tracking the Milestones 77

Chapter 9: The Power of Journaling 85

Chapter 10: Counting the Streak — The Power of Habit-Tracking Apps 87

Chapter 11: How to Shape Your Habits — Social Accountability — Try This With Your Friends! 89

Chapter 12: Don't Over Do It! 93

Chapter 13: Conclusion — Embrace Toothbrush Yoga, Transform Your Life 99

Share Your Toothbrush Yoga Journey: Reviews and Testimonials 101

Toothbrush Yoga Pose Index 103

APPENDIX 183

About the Author 193

Preface

Welcome to Toothbrush Yoga — a new approach to incorporating yoga into your daily life, without the need to head to a yoga class or don expensive gear. I invite you not to a studio, but to your kitchen, living room and bathroom. Toothbrush Yoga is for you if you can see the physical and mental health benefits of incorporating yoga into your life, but struggle to find the time (or money) to get to a yoga class. Or, if you just can't figure out how to make yoga a habit.

The true beauty of Toothbrush Yoga lies in its ability to dissolve the rigid compartments that have been constructed around your daily activities. You don't need to isolate it into a specific time or space, away from the demands of work, family, or personal time. Toothbrush Yoga is about demonstrating that you *can* bring yoga into your life as easily as brushing your teeth. In fact, the whole point of this book is to look at the habits you *already have* and use them as opportunities to build in yoga throughout your day. A little and often.

This is a practical book. Using the latest neuroscience and psychology research, I look at how new habits are formed and give you the tools to help you succeed in expanding them to include yoga poses. I take you through a typical day, looking at the habits and routines we all have. Rather than suggesting spending hours in the yoga studio, I help you identify those habits as opportunities where we can bring yoga to you. In the context of this book, these moments translate into poses which could be as little as 30-120 seconds — the time it takes to boil a kettle or floss your teeth.

Yoga is not about touching your toes, it's about what you learn on the way down.

Jigar Gor

In the book, I provide you with a 10-step process including examples of how I have achieved this myself, including pictures showcasing my daily routine so you can see how easy it is. I won't ask you to overhaul your lifestyle; instead, I'll show you how to infuse your existing habits with the grace of yoga.

You absolutely do not need to have prior yoga experience to start Toothbrush Yoga! The comprehensive Yoga Pose Index, towards the back of the book, provides a fully illustrated, step-by-step guide detailing 47 standing, sitting, kneeling, and lying poses, how to achieve them, variations to each pose, as well as any cautions and modifications associated with each pose, so you can quickly refer to it as you start to bring in yoga and see how a pose should be done. Explore 40 concise YouTube Shorts, each lasting less than a minute, providing step-by-step demonstrations on how to achieve the yoga poses.

I hope that this book can set you on a transformative journey, bringing yoga and all its health benefits into your day-to-day life, one moment at a time. Maybe too, this is something you can share with your family and start to nurture great habits with your kids, or even with older parents. Prepare to witness the fusion of ancient wisdom and modern behavioural science to discover the extraordinary power of mindful habits one set of clean teeth at a time.

We are what we repeatedly do. Excellence, then, is not an act, but a habit.

Aristotle

Introducing Toothbrush Yoga — Tiny Habits, Transformational Results

If you've picked up this book, you're likely to be an individual navigating a hectic lifestyle, seeking a practical and achievable approach to integrating yoga seamlessly into your daily routines. Whether you're a busy professional, a parent with limited time, a student managing academic demands, someone at any life stage recognising the importance of well-being, or maybe you just want to get more familiar with your toes again, this guide caters to diverse audiences. It's designed for those of you who yearn for a holistic and sustainable fitness solution, allowing you to harness the power of habit stacking for improved physical, mental, and emotional well-being.

Perhaps you're here because you desire more than fleeting progress; you crave lasting change that seamlessly integrates into your life, effortlessly becoming a part of who you are. Good news, you've picked up the right book. Welcome to the world of Toothbrush Yoga, where the pursuit of holistic well-being meets the science of sustainable habit formation.

Every action you take is a vote for the type of person you wish to become.

James Clear — Atomic Habits

This is not your typical guide, promising enlightenment through hours of meditation or impossibly contorted poses. This is an exploration of yoga in its most accessible, adaptable, and simplistic form fused with ground-breaking neuroscience and behavioural research.

If you've ever felt the allure of yoga but found the conventional path too daunting, or if you're simply curious about having greater suppleness by leveraging the habits that you have already ingrained, this is the place to start. Prepare to embrace yoga not as a distant goal but as an integral part of your here and now.

One of the most remarkable aspects of Toothbrush Yoga lies in its adaptability. Within the hustle and bustle of your life, priorities and routines often shift like the changing seasons. Life is ever-changing, and so frequently, is your fitness regime. With Toothbrush Yoga, you're not bound by the limitations of a fixed schedule or a specific location.

No matter how busy life gets or where your adventures take you, Toothbrush Yoga is designed to be your steadfast companion. Whether you're on a tropical beach, navigating a bustling city, or simply at home, your ability to practice yoga isn't confined to a specific time or place.

By integrating yoga into daily rituals like washing up or waiting for your coffee to brew, Toothbrush Yoga moulds itself to the contours of your life. It is your practice, done your way. Feel free to modify poses, incorporate your favourite stretches, or adapt the practice to accommodate your specific needs. It's about finding what resonates with you and allowing yoga to flow harmoniously with your life, fitting seamlessly into your daily rituals — a way that celebrates progress over perfection, mindfulness over monotony, and gentle persistence over intense effort. Together, we will infuse the secrets of habit formation with the transformative power of yoga, unlocking the power of lasting change with minimal effort and maximum impact.

Change is the result of all true learning.

Leo Buscaglia

Bite-Sized Yoga — Less than 2 Minutes

In the vast breadth of yoga, there exists a wide spectrum of styles, from the dynamic flows of Vinyasa to the precise postures of Hatha, the vigorous athleticism of Ashtanga to the meditative embrace of Kundalini. Toothbrush Yoga isn't focused on a particular style, just simple poses, (also known as asanas).

As you turn the pages, you won't find complex Sanskrit terminology or intimidating poses. Instead, you'll embark on a delightful approach which is as easy as lying in bed.... which is where many of the poses can be performed!

Toothbrush Yoga is not focused on a grand performance of contorted dynamic sequences or the graceful dance of sun salutations demanding hours of practice. There aren't hours spent on the mat, just mere seconds, or minutes. In the context of this book, these moments translate into poses which could be as little as 30-120 seconds — the time it takes to boil a kettle or floss your teeth. A humble duration, yet profoundly transformative.

Toothbrush Yoga, in its essence, is about the art of holding a pose, finding serenity in each breath, and allowing the body to surrender, inch by inch, and then getting on with the rest of your day.

Am I Too Old?

You might think yoga isn't for you, or that it has an age bias because you've been bombarded with images of young women bent double, but this isn't the case. In the Yoga Alliance's 2016 study of the 36 million US yoga participants, there was an even distribution of age ranges, 18-29 — 19%, 30-39 —

23%, 40-49 — 20%, 50-59 — 17% and 60+ -27%. I've listed the sources for my research in the Appendix (for this and all other reference points you'll see, so you are welcome to check for yourself. I can tell you from personal experience though, that a more advanced age is not an issue.

Age is not a barrier. I started at 50!

All you need to do is to listen to your body (which is true at any age). Take it slow, do nothing that hurts and adapts each pose in the way that works for your body.

What Does Yoga Do for You? — It's Way More Than Just Stretching

The physical benefits of yoga are astounding, reaching far beyond the common misconception of it merely being a stretching exercise. Yoga, in its myriad forms, enhances elasticity, strengthens muscles, improves balance, and increases endurance.

But its influence extends deeper, massaging internal organs, and promoting their optimal functioning. It regulates blood pressure, enhances respiratory efficiency, and aids in digestion. Furthermore, yoga boosts the immune system, fostering overall health and well-being.

Yoga teaches us to cure what need not be endured and endure what cannot be cured.

B.K.S. Iyengar

An article published in the UK newspaper The Times quoted several research papers relating to the benefits of stretching. The article reported that "performing a series of leg stretches five times a week had an anti-ageing effect on the arteries of healthy people" and "the benefits of stretching extend beyond blood vessels to our nervous system as well, which makes it a great addition to help patients slow disease progression."

By decoding the algorithms of your cumulative behavioural routines and embracing Toothbrush Yoga as an inherent part of your everyday moments you can help your overall well-being in many ways:

- **Stimulating your deep tissue** — Toothbrush Yoga targets deep connective tissues, including ligaments, tendons, and fascia. Poses are held, allowing muscles to relax and lengthen gradually. This prolonged stretching is designed to lead to improved bendability over time.

- **Releasing stress and aiding relaxation** — Toothbrush Yoga emphasises relaxation and deep breathing, promoting the activation of the parasympathetic nervous system, inducing a state of calm and reducing stress and anxiety.
- **Improving joint health** — your practice will help to maintain joint mobility, reducing the risk of joint-related issues as one ages. It encourages synovial fluid production, which nourishes joints.
- **Deepening mindfulness and meditation** — in addition to physical well-being Toothbrush Yoga encourages a meditative mindset, as you hold poses for extended periods, which provides the opportunity to engage in mindfulness, self-awareness, and an inward focus.
- **Stimulating organs and improving circulation** — certain poses compress and stimulate specific organs, which is said to enhance organ function and improve blood circulation.
- **Preventing injury and improving rehabilitation** — the gentle nature of Toothbrush Yoga makes it suitable for injury prevention and rehabilitation. It allows you to work on your mobility without putting excessive stress on joints and muscles. More generally, yoga is renowned for its ability to ease chronic pain, making it an invaluable tool for those suffering from conditions like arthritis or lower back pain. Through gentle, controlled movements and breathwork, yoga eases muscular tension, offering relief and promoting healing.

If you could reap those benefits, with minimal disruption to your everyday life, would you?

So how is it possible to bring all of these benefits into your life?

This is where Toothbrush Yoga comes in. By infusing the art of yoga into your everyday existence, seamlessly merging it with tasks as mundane as brushing your teeth or reading a book — perhaps this one!

The key to Toothbrush Yoga lies in the transformative power of yoga when combined with the transformational power of habit. Merging the wisdom of ancient yogic practices and practical insights from the wonderful world of neuroscience and behavioural research.

Welcome to Toothbrush Yoga — where Tiny Habits turn into Transformative Results.

Your beliefs become your thoughts, your thoughts become your words, your words become your actions, your actions become your habits, your habits become your values, and your values become your destiny.

Mahatma Gandhi

My Path to Becoming a Toothbrush Yogi

For my New Year's resolution on the 1st of January 2010, I signed up for a 10km run, which was taking place that May. I headed down to the January sales and bought myself a new pair of gleaming running shoes.

I dedicated myself to an 8-week beginners 10km programme and, three times a week, I would lace up my new trainers and head out, through the snow and rain on those cold, dark winter nights, pounding out the steps, believing that it would only take 21 days for my new running "habit" to kick in.

My first 10km distance was clocked up slightly earlier than the 8 weeks I had planned for. It was now the end of February; I had another 11 weeks before the race started!

I hated the mind-numbing monotony and endless breathlessness that a 55-minute 10km run took. It eventually became less physically taxing as my fitness improved, but as soon as I crossed the race line in May, my trainers didn't see the light of day again.

What happened to the 21 days to form a habit?? I'd clocked up a total of 57 pavement thrashing runs over the previous 19 weeks. Surely I should be a happy regular runner by now?

The Myth of 21 Days: Debunking the Truth about Habit Formation

The 21 days to form a habit originated from a book by Dr Maxwell Maltz in the 1960s, called Psycho-cybernetics. The plastic surgeon turned psychologist determined that his patients grew accustomed to their physical changes, be they amputation or plastic surgery in 21 days. This was then extended to pretty much everything else creating the 21-day habit myth. I'm not sure accepting that you have an irreversible physical change to your body is the best way to determine how long a habit is formed, but somehow this turned into folklore.

'It usually requires a minimum of about 21 days to effect any perceptible change in a mental image. Following plastic surgery, it takes about 21 days for the average patient to get used to his new face. When an arm or leg is amputated the "phantom limb" persists for about 21 days. People must live in a new house for about three weeks before it begins to "seem like home". These, and many other commonly observed phenomena tend to show that it requires a minimum of about 21 days for an old mental image to dissolve and a new one to jell.'

Research published in The European Journal of Social Psychology shows that there isn't a magical number for habit formation, with timespans for new habit formation from 18 to 254 days, which averaged out to 66 days. Logically, the simpler the habit, the quicker it was to assimilate.

Shifting from Motivation to Identity — Unlocking the Key to Sustainable Change

The second problem, and undoubtedly the biggest hurdle, was that at no point did I actually want to *be* a runner. I hadn't changed my identity from a non-runner into someone who runs. Whilst I'd developed a new "habit" of running 3 times a week, at no point did I *want* to be a runner, it was simply a personal goal that I'd set myself.

As Dr Maltz went on to say in his book, *'Our self-image and our habits tend to go together. Change one and you will automatically change the other.'* The so-called habit that I'd developed, wasn't tied to my identity, it only lasted as long as my motivation endured, which was the 10km finish line!

The allure of motivation is undeniable. It sparks our enthusiasm, propels us into action, and whispers promises of a better tomorrow.

> *If anything has been learned from the graveyard of abandoned New Year resolutions, it's that motivation is a fleeting companion. Its flame, once burning brightly, can dwindle into mere embers, leaving us stranded in the vast expanse of our ambitions.*

Imagine motivation as a sprinter in a marathon race. At the starting line, it surges forward with incredible speed, leaving you in awe of its power. But just like any sprinter, motivation exhausts itself. When the initial excitement fades, the real challenge begins. This is where identity becomes the marathon runner of your personal development. Had I adopted the identity of a runner, I wouldn't have needed my motivation to propel me beyond the finishing line. I would have continued to go running, maybe not as often post-race, but even if I didn't don my trainers as often, I would still be running.

American research has found that only 9% of Americans who make a New Year's Resolution complete them. Of the 91% that fail, 23% quit by the end of the first week, and 43% quit by the end of January. Of those people who gave up drinking, smoking, overeating, learning a new language etc on the 1st of January, how many actually identified as a non-smoker, non-drinkers, healthy eaters, or a speaker of a new language?

Building your identity is akin to constructing a sturdy bridge between your aspirations and your actions. It's a process that acknowledges the transient nature of motivation and instead relies on recognising initially at first who you want to be, and through consistency, repetition, and small, incremental steps, the person you have become. While motivation may ebb and flow, habits, once ingrained, become the reliable foundation upon which you can build lasting change. Whilst I had achieved my personal goal of running a 10km race, for my 'habit' to persist I would have needed to *want to be* a runner.

To change who you want to be is therefore intrinsically linked to what you do and vice versa. Your identity is like a magnet, pulling you back to your habitual behaviours. Consider this for a moment: an individual who sees themselves as a runner is far more likely to establish a consistent running programme, rather than one goal. It's not merely about the actions you take; it's about the person you believe you are during those actions.

Your identity is your most valuable possession. Protect it.

Elastigirl (The Incredibles)

Who You Are Shapes What You Do

In the summer of 2012, I was playing my usual game of Tuesday night 5-a-side football when I went into a tackle that was about to change my life. I limped off the pitch thinking it would be nothing more than a couple of weeks on the touchline only to later discover that I'd sliced off a significant chuck of my meniscus (it's the soft, rubbery disk that helps protect your bones when you move. Imagine it as a comfy pillow between your knee bones, allowing them to glide smoothly without bumping into each other).

As I sat in front of the knee surgeon, he ran me through his thoughts. "We could operate and there's a 40% chance that we'll improve your knee, there is a 40% chance that it will be exactly the same and a 20% chance that it will get worse." So, there's a 60% chance it will be the same or worse I thought (not really what I was expecting to hear). "Or you could do some strengthening exercises on your leg, which will realign your kneecap and may well do the job."

Guess which option I took?

Playing football was *extremely* important to me, I had expected to be playing well into my 60s. I saw myself as a footballer. Without football I was miserable and without exercise, I became sedentary and at risk of drinking too much and putting on weight. Not playing sports was having a big impact on my overall well-being.

I'd reached the tender age of 40, and I'd never played a season of 11-a-side adult football. It was something that, until the opportunity was taken away from me, I'd never really thought about doing, so the outcome I wanted to achieve was to play at least one season of Sunday League Football.

I needed to lengthen my hamstrings as well as strengthen my vastus medialis (the bulgy muscle by your kneecap on the inside of your leg when you straighten it) to realign my kneecap. I set myself two goals, to touch my toes, and to be able to do 50 one-legged knee squats with weights.

The approach I adopted was to practice a Forward Fold Pose (I didn't know it was called that or even that it was a yoga pose), every morning when I brushed my teeth, and I would do squats when I brushed my teeth at night.

What I hadn't realised was that I was forming a habit, nurturing it with each rotation of my toothbrush. I've adhered to this routine for more than a decade, both in the morning and evening, with remarkable consistency. That equates to roughly 7,300 iterations.

If for any reason I skip the morning, there is always the evening, and if I happen to skip a whole day, there is always the next day or the one after that. I will continue to brush my teeth for as long as I'm alive and as long as I clean my teeth, I'll be doing my exercises.

Week by week, month by month, I slowly increased the length of my hamstrings, to the point where I can now comfortably place my hands flat on the floor, and, having discovered yoga, I'm working towards my long-term goal of touching my head on my shins. I'm still quite some way off, and there is a reasonable chance that I might not make it, but that consistent action has meant that I haven't had a hamstring injury for years, and my knee, has never given me a single issue since. It meant that I could achieve my objective of playing Sunday League football and I'm still playing 11-a-side Sunday League Football in my fifties.

Reshaping Identity — Becoming a Yogi

When I took some time out from the Rat Race in 2022, my girlfriend Rachel and I travelled through Southeast Asia. I had the misfortune of breaking a tooth in Chiang Mai, Northern Thailand, and had to hang around for a week between my first and second appointments. At a loose end, we decided to head out into the countryside and experience a Yoga Retreat for a few days at True Nature Yoga & Meditation Homestay Retreat.

My prior yogic experience was having, under duress, attended a couple of virtual yoga classes with Rachel during the COVID lockdowns. Not knowing my Cat from my Dog poses, off I went with limited expectations.

As the founders, Ning and Adam, welcomed us into their sanctuary, I was captivated by the serenity of the mountainside and the warm hospitality of our hosts, along with their delightful cats and dogs.

The retreat unfolded with immersive yoga and meditation classes, both invigorating and calming, guided by Adam. I discovered the profound benefits of yoga, not just in physical elasticity but in fostering mental clarity and a sense of harmony. The connection with nature became a central theme, evident in every aspect of the retreat with the serene environment providing opportunities for introspection, whether unwinding in a hammock with a book or exploring the nearby waterfall and jungles.

> *Yoga is not about reaching perfection, but about embracing the imperfections and finding peace within them in your journey.*

True Nature wasn't just a physical journey; it was a soulful exploration that left an indelible mark on my perspective of well-being, harmony, and the profound potential of yoga. The retreat's ethos, focusing on simplicity, connection with nature, and the nourishing practices of yoga and meditation, resonated deeply and set the stage for a newfound passion and direction in my life. Inspired by this enriching experience, the idea of becoming a yoga teacher was born, and my identity was becoming reshaped.

As I continued my travels, the seed of Toothbrush Yoga began to sprout in my mind. The lightbulb moment occurred when I picked up the book "Atomic Habits" at one of the hostels. In the pages of James Clear's work, I stumbled upon the concept of habit stacking (I'll dig into that a bit later), a term that perfectly encapsulated what I had intuitively done with my toothbrushing routine.

The synergy between habit transformation and yogic practice became clear. It wasn't just about performing yoga poses during daily rituals; it was a harmonious fusion of habit-building principles and the profound benefits of yoga. The ordinary act of brushing my teeth became a gateway to a more intentional, holistic approach to well-being.

The purpose of Yoga is not to become someone else; it's about awakening to who you truly are on the journey of self-realisation.

This recognition took root, and as Rachel and I made our way from country to country, I delved into understanding the potential of harnessing the power of habits. The synergy between my habit stacking revelation and the yogic path paved the way for a holistic approach that extended beyond the mat.

This newfound awareness coincided with a pivotal decision — signing up for the 200-hour Yoga Teacher Training on the picturesque island of Nusa Lembongan in Bali, Indonesia. In the same way, I saw my toothbrushing habit saving my footballing ambitions, I could see how the benefits of yoga could maintain my physical vitality well into the later stages of my life. The decision to become a yoga teacher wasn't therefore merely a professional pursuit; it marked the intentional shaping of a new identity, a commitment to a lifelong journey of well-being — one that acknowledged the transformative power of intentional habits and the timeless wisdom of yoga.

The concept of Toothbrush Yoga evolved beyond a personal routine to become a transformative practice, where everyday rituals seamlessly integrated with yoga poses.

My identity has now morphed into that of a Yogi, and my outcome is to develop and maintain flexibility and mobility throughout my life as I continue to age. I want to be actively mobile up to the end of my existence, whenever that might be.

Yoga is the habit of serenity in motion.

Whilst I do attend traditional yoga classes on an irregular basis, my own practice framework is based on adopting yoga poses throughout the day wherever I am and whatever I am doing. The balance between my goals and identity ensures that my habits are not fleeting achievements but enduring reflections of my commitment to the outcome I have set for myself in terms of lifelong well-being.

What I learnt from my failed running habit was that aligning my identity with the habits that I wished to cultivate was the foundation of lasting change. This book is not just about practicing yoga when you're in bed reading a book; or watching TV, it's about becoming a person who practices yoga effortlessly, seamlessly integrating it into the very fabric of your daily life. It's about being someone whose identity is about cherishing suppleness and overall well-being.

In the chapters that follow, I share the essence of my transformative experience, weaving together the lessons learned from my yoga teacher journey and the research I have gathered in the science of habit formation to bring you Toothbrush Yoga.

The Toothbrush Yoga framework will provide you with a step-by-step guide to enable you to hack into your unconscious mind's autopilot software and prompt you to practice a particular pose, with minimal effort. The smallest actions, when practiced consistently, can create seismic shifts in your well-being enabling you to evolve your autopilot into the compass that leads you towards a new destination.

Let this shared wisdom be a source of inspiration, motivating you to adopt a new identity, explore your potential, and manifest your desired outcomes. What can you expect from this book?

Chapter 1: The Triad of Transformation: Outcomes, Identity, and Goals

This chapter embarks on an exploration of the outcomes you seek, your identity and the goals that underpin your development. Examining how your self-perception influences your habits as you discover the power of aligning your outcomes with your identity and goals. How your habits shape your identity, and your identity reinforces your habits, creating a virtuous, transformative loop that propels you toward a more mindful, balanced, and harmonious existence.

Chapter 2: The Hidden Forces — Decoding the Mechanisms of Habits

Delves deep into the intricate world of habits, exploring how they invisibly shape your life and behaviours. Defining what a habit flow is and how cues, cravings, responses, and rewards are the unconscious controls of your autopilot.

Habits are like financial capital – forming one today is an investment for the future.

Chapter 3: Hijacking the Habit Flow

Dives into the core methodology of Toothbrush Yoga and the introduction of habit stacking and its transformative potential. It details the technique of how to interrupt your habit flow, enabling you to make Toothbrush Yoga, not just a new habit, but a lifestyle change.

Chapter 4: My Toothbrush Yoga Framework — Morning Ritual

In this chapter I lift the lid on my own morning rituals, detailing how I have crafted a lasting lifestyle change with minimal effort and maximum impact, effortlessly weaving flexibility, balance, and mindfulness into my daily existence. I uncover the prompts and poses that my morning practice is based on, from the moment I wake, through to stepping out of the door.

Build habits, build yourself – they are the foundation of personal growth.

Chapter 5: Toothbrush Yoga at Work/Study

Work and study environments often demand prolonged periods of sitting/standing and concentration. You are introduced to Toothbrush Yoga exercises that can be practiced during the workday, combating the frequently sedentary challenges of the modern workplace. Techniques for practicing Toothbrush Yoga while standing or sitting, typing, or reading are shared, empowering you to infuse moments of mindfulness into your busy schedules. By incorporating these subtle yet effective exercises, you can reduce stress, improve posture, and enhance focus, creating a harmonious balance between work demands and personal well-being.

Progress isn't about flawlessness; it's the beautiful art of embracing imperfection along the way.

Chapter 6: Toothbrush Yoga in Everyday Tasks

Yoga is not confined to the mat; it can permeate every aspect of daily life. In this chapter, you will rediscover the ordinary as extraordinary by integrating Toothbrush Yoga into everyday tasks. From washing dishes, scrolling on your device, or watching TV, you are introduced to Toothbrush Yoga poses that enhance balance and limberness. Mundane chores can be transformed into opportunities for mindful movement, allowing you to cultivate presence and grace in your daily activities. By infusing these tasks with Toothbrush Yoga, you can navigate life's demands with calmness and poise, fostering a sense of contentment in the midst of routine.

Chapter 7: Toothbrush Yoga in Evening Rituals

The evening marks a transition from the hustle and bustle of the day to a quieter, more introspective time. In this chapter, you are guided on how to integrate Toothbrush Yoga into your evening rituals, fostering a sense of tranquillity and relaxation. By infusing your evening routines with Toothbrush Yoga, you can create a serene environment, helping you to unwind, let go of stress, and prepare for a restful night's sleep. Through these practices, you can embrace the evening as a sacred time for self-care and rejuvenation, ensuring you wake up refreshed and renewed the next day.

Chapter 8: Your Toothbrush Yoga Framework

Your own Toothbrush Yoga journey begins here creating your own Toothbrush Yoga framework. Starting with your desired outcomes and the identity you want to adopt, you will then map out the what, the where, the when and how you intend to practice Toothbrush Yoga. And finally, setting the goals that you want to track your progress with.

A daily stretch is a habit, a lifetime of flexibility is the reward.

Chapter 9: The Power of Journaling

Journaling plays a pivotal role within the Toothbrush Yoga framework, offering profound benefits supported by research and real-life experiences. A study published in The British Journal of Health Psychology found that 91% of participants who defined their intention to exercise by writing down when and where they would exercise ended up following through.

Therefore, tracking your Toothbrush Yoga journey isn't just a record-keeping exercise; it's a powerful tool that transforms subtle progress into palpable motivation and achievable actions. The very act of tracking progress creates momentum and is a habit in itself. As you see your progress accumulate over time, you're inspired to continue.

Maintaining a record of your journey, in whatever form that suits you, visual, written, or simply mental enables you to reflect on how each pose makes you feel, both physically and mentally. Documenting your progress can create a tangible record of your journey, highlighting the consistency and fostering a sense of achievement.

Chapter 10: Counting the Streak — The Power of Habit-Tracking Apps

This is where ancient wisdom meets modern technology, and your smartphone becomes a portal to wellness. With the help of these apps introduced in the chapter, your phone can offer notifications that gently prompt you to practice, as well as provide visual progress indicators and streak counters which serve as constant reminders of your dedication, fuelling your determination.

Chapter 11: How to Shape Your Habits — Social Accountability — Try This With Your Friends!

In the dynamic landscape of habit formation, community and social connections play a vital role. This chapter explores the strength of shared goals and mutual encouragement. Delve into the enriching world of social accountability, where your Toothbrush Yoga practice becomes a collective endeavour. Learn how shared commitment and supportive partnerships elevate your motivation, making the journey toward wellness a shared adventure. This chapter empowers you to engage with others, fostering a network of support that amplifies your progress and enriches your Toothbrush Yoga experience.

If you believe you can change – if you make it a habit – the change becomes real.

Chapter 12: Don't Over Do It!

This is a gentle reminder that progress in your Toothbrush Yoga journey is about consistency, not intensity. Here, you will explore the nuances of moderation and how it's key to sustainability. Discover the fine line between challenging yourself and respecting your body's limits. This chapter will guide you in understanding when to push your boundaries and when to grant yourself the grace of rest. Embrace this chapter as your compass, ensuring your Toothbrush Yoga practice remains a source of joy and vitality.

Chapter 13: Conclusion — Embrace Toothbrush Yoga, Transform Your Life

In the conclusion, I revisit the transformative power of integrating Toothbrush Yoga into everyday routines. You are encouraged to continue your Toothbrush Yoga journey, celebrating your achievements, and embracing the ongoing process of self-discovery and growth. The conclusion reinforces the idea that small, consistent efforts lead to profound and lasting changes, empowering you to continue mindful habits and inspiring others to join you on the path to holistic wellness.

Toothbrush Yoga Pose Index

Perhaps the most useful area in this book is this comprehensive and detailed index featuring 47 standing, seated, kneeling, and lying poses, including pictures, (links to videos in the eBook) and helpful hints. These poses are referenced throughout the previous chapters and serve as the ultimate guide on which to base your Toothbrush Yoga practice upon. Each pose is accompanied by annotated images showing the poses, step-by-step instructions on how to achieve them, variations to the poses and any cautions and modifications you need to be aware of.

As you navigate this book, approach each chapter with an open heart and a curious mind. Focus on who you want to become, engage with the exercises, reflect on the prompts, and honour your journey. Remember, this book is your guide, but the transformation lies within you. Embrace the teachings, practice with dedication, be mindful about who you want to become and let the wisdom of Toothbrush Yoga illuminate your path to well-being.

Believe nothing, no matter where you read it or who has said it unless it agrees with your own reason and your own common sense.

Buddha

Chapter 1: The Triad of Transformation: Outcomes, Identity, and Goals

In the heart of the Toothbrush Yoga framework lies a powerful triad: outcomes, identity/beliefs, and goals. These three underlying principles act as the building blocks of your transformational journey.

Your outcomes define what you are looking to achieve, serving as the guiding compass for your practice. Whether it's increased mobility, improved balance, or overall well-being, clarifying your desired outcomes provides a clear direction for your journey.

Your identity and beliefs wrap around your outcomes and play a pivotal role in shaping your habit transformation. Embracing the identity of a Toothbrush Yogi involves not just the physical practice but a shift in mindset. As you weave yoga into your daily life, consider the beliefs you hold about yourself and your capabilities. Are you open to growth, resilience, and the potential for positive change?

Your goals act as the stepping stones that mark your progress along the way. These aren't just lofty aspirations but tangible milestones that keep you on track. Setting specific, measurable, and achievable goals ensures that your Toothbrush Yoga journey is not just a concept but a dynamic, evolving practice.

Together, these elements form a cohesive framework, providing structure and purpose to your Toothbrush Yoga practice. As you delve into the poses and rituals, let the triad of outcomes, identity/beliefs, and goals be your guiding companions, propelling you toward a more limber, balanced, and harmonious self. Let's delve into each one.

Outcomes: Defining Your Destination

There is a common misunderstanding about outcomes and goals. Goals are tangible, measurable objectives. They provide direction but might lack depth, are often narrowly focused, and frequently revolve around specific achievements. Outcomes, on the other hand, encompass a broader, more profound perspective. They not only define what you aim to achieve but also shape the very essence of your identity.

Desired outcomes are the dreams; habits are the ladders to reach them.

When I talk about outcomes in the context of Toothbrush Yoga, I'm delving into the layers which sit beneath the surface aspirations. It's not just about losing weight or becoming more agile; it's about the person you're evolving into throughout this process. Your outcome isn't merely a number on a scale or a milestone in your yoga journey; it's the essence of your transformation.

Outcomes encapsulate the emotional, psychological, and even spiritual facets of your aspirations. They intertwine with your identity, becoming an integral part of who you are. For example, a goal might be to practice a headstand in yoga, but the outcome is the confidence, strength, and balance that a headstand signifies in your life. Instead of setting grand yoga goals, this book will enable you to develop your own daily Toothbrush Yoga framework based on the outcomes you desire.

Your journey needs to begin with a clear understanding of the outcomes you wish to achieve. Let's say your outcome is enhanced mobility and flexibility. This outcome becomes your guiding star, illuminating the path ahead. It's not just about physical prowess; it's about reclaiming the freedom to move effortlessly, embracing every moment with vitality.

Identity/Beliefs: Shaping Your Self-Perception

Everyone wears many identities — fathers, mothers, children, grandparents, job or profession, politically left, right or centre, religious or atheist, savers or spenders, sports team supporters…..the list is almost endless. These labels inform the beliefs that govern our behaviours, the lenses through which we perceive the world, influencing our thoughts, emotions, and actions. Beliefs play a pivotal role in shaping our habits and, ultimately, the outcomes we strive for, as well as the goals that we set for ourselves.

Many of the truths that we cling to depend on our point of view.

Yoda

Identity Unveiled: How Toothbrush Yoga Deepened My Sense of Self and Beliefs

I've come to believe in the power of small, consistent actions, which align seamlessly with my philosophy of incremental growth. Toothbrush Yoga's emphasis on habit transformation resonates with my conviction that lasting change often begins with subtle shifts in daily routines. The concept of habit stacking, as outlined in Atomic Habits, became a revelation, intertwining effortlessly with my existing belief in the potential of micro-habits to create substantial alterations to my behaviours.

I am aware that my optimal state of well-being is closely tied to engaging in regular physical exercise, contributing to a happier version of myself. A resilient mind and a physically capable body are intertwined aspects of my personal well-being. The synergy of mental strength and physical dexterity creates a foundation for emotional balance. Embracing the interconnectedness of physical, mental, and emotional wellness aligns with my holistic philosophy toward health. In harmony with Toothbrush

Yoga's recognition of the mind-body connection, I uphold the belief that genuine wellness transcends the confines of the physical body.

Change your habits, transform your identity.

Becoming a Toothbrush Yogi has reinforced my identity as someone who values mindfulness in every aspect of life. It has elevated my commitment to adaptability, viewing challenges as opportunities for growth.

As I embraced the principles of continuous growth and resilience within the Toothbrush Yoga identity, I found a harmonious blend with my personal ethos. The recognition that setbacks are stepping stones to progress aligns with my belief in embracing adversity as a catalyst for personal development.

The most effective way to change your habits is to focus not on what you want to achieve, but on who you wish to become.

James Clear — Atomic Habits

In essence, my journey into Toothbrush Yoga has not only validated my existing beliefs but has magnified and refined my identity. The alignment has created a synergy where the principles of Toothbrush Yoga seamlessly merge with the core values and convictions that have shaped my outlook on well-being, growth, and mindful living.

Who Do You Want to Become?

I assume that you've chosen this book because you'd like to achieve a lasting change.

What is that?

Are you a busy professional seeking to reclaim some health and fitness in your life?

A parent with neither the time nor energy at the end of the day for a fitness class?

Someone acknowledging the passage of time and yearning to regain mobility and suppleness?

Who do you need to become to affect this change?

What are your desired outcomes for life and who do you need to become to achieve this?

In the pursuit of your new identity, habits will form a powerful part of how it is shaped, moulding you into the person you aspire to be. Simultaneously, your identity will also reinforce your habits, creating a virtuous, transformative loop that propels you toward a more mindful, balanced, and harmonious existence.

By changing what you do; you set out on a pathway to become the person you aspire to be. By repeatedly performing the habits of your desired identity, you will bridge the gap between aspiration and reality.

What is your identity and what beliefs are aligned with your desired outcomes?

It's important to cultivate beliefs that empower you, such as believing in your body's ability to adapt and grow. Embrace the identity of a resilient, adaptable individual who thrives on challenges. Believe in your body's innate capacity to improve — try and visualise yourself as a dedicated yogi, resilient in the face of stretching challenges, and confident in your ability to achieve your goals.

It doesn't matter how deep into a pose you go — what does matter is who you are when you get there.

Max Storm

Goals: Milestones of Progress

When embarking on any long journey, signposts provide the reassurance that you are heading in the right direction. Goals are the signposts of habit formation, providing you with direction, but as you've seen from my own running experience, goals are just one aspect of lasting change.

Goals serve as the stepping stones toward your desired outcomes and can be a powerful ally when it comes to developing habits.

Because they are specific, once you have achieved a goal, there is no compulsion to continue. Lose 5kg of weight, run a 10km race — once the goal has been achieved, you are likely to move on to the next thing and gradually the habit that promoted the motivation fades. Setting a goal, such as achieving a desired result, can be motivating, but it must be balanced with a deeper understanding of the process of habit change.

The Negative Side of Goals

The downside of goals is that on their own they can also have a negative side effect, creating a binary conflict: either you accomplish your goal and succeed, or you fall short and fail, inevitably losing motivation.

The overall size of the goal can often detract from its purpose. Run a marathon, lose 20kg, climb a mountain, stop smoking. If the goal is too big, the effort to achieve it is also too great. These can be daunting goals and just feel unachievable.

Eating the Elephant

Habit transformation can often resemble the monumental task of eating an elephant. The enormity of the challenge can be overwhelming, leaving you wondering where to start. But as the saying goes, "How do you eat an elephant? One bite at a time." This age-old wisdom encapsulates the essence of Toothbrush Yoga — by breaking down colossal goals into manageable, bite-sized pieces.

> *Just as one cannot consume an elephant in a single gulp, transformative change doesn't happen overnight.*

By focusing on one bite at a time, one habit at a time, you can navigate the intricate path of habit formation. Embracing the metaphor of eating the elephant, you embark on a journey of self-discovery, transformation, and lifelong wellness.

So, the key is to start with small, manageable changes that reflect your desired identity. These could be as simple as practicing mindful breathing when performing a Corpse Pose before you fall asleep. Small changes, when consistently practiced, pave the way for significant transformation. As you step through this book you will learn where the opportunities are in your daily life to introduce Toothbrush Yoga poses, how you develop the prompts to remind you to practice and finally what poses might suit the situation.

Going back to our example outcomes — if you desire enhanced flexibility and mobility for life, your goals might include touching your toes comfortably and balancing in a particular pose for a defined duration. Each goal is a milestone representing progress towards that bigger picture.

Ensure that your goals align with actions attainable within your current lifestyle. Make small, incremental changes to your existing habits that propel you toward the future version of yourself.

This blend of goal-based motivation and identity-based commitment creates a holistic approach, ensuring that your habits are not just tasks but a reflection of who you are becoming.

Each goal achieved reinforces your identity, which brings you closer to your desired outcomes. It showcases the power of aligning outcomes, identity, and goals, creating a harmonious synergy that propels you towards your aspirations.

Setting goals is the first step in turning the invisible into the visible.

Tony Robbins

Chapter 2: The Hidden Forces — Decoding the Mechanisms of Habits

In the bustling canvas of your life, habits paint the most intricate strokes. They're the daily rituals that shape your existence, often without you even noticing. From the way you brush your teeth to driving a car, habit is the autopilot of your life, guiding you through your routines, and influencing your behaviours, thoughts, and emotions.

Imagine *your* autopilot as a piece of sophisticated software constantly running in the background of your mind, conserving your mental energy, and allowing you to navigate your day with minimal conscious effort. Your autopilot, over the course of your life, creates shortcuts to automate as many tasks as possible to minimise the involvement of your brain.

The power of habit lies in its quiet persistence.

Scientists from the McGovern Institute have made a significant discovery. During the initial stages of learning a new task, the frontal lobe and basal ganglia of the brain are notably active, engaging in complex calculations. These brain regions collaborate to link behaviours with thoughts, emotions, and, crucially, motor movements. The research at McGovern experimented with rats, who were exposed to a maze and trained to explore it looking for a reward. During the repetitive action of navigating the maze, the rat's brains optimised the process resulting in fewer neurons being necessary to accomplish each task. In essence, the more a task is practiced, the smoother its execution becomes. This phenomenon occurs because the behaviour becomes ingrained in the brain, etched in the form of motor movements, making it increasingly effortless to perform. The idea that the brain optimises processes is further proven when the reward is removed, and the behaviour still exists. Bizarrely even when the reward is tampered with (and even contaminated), the behaviour is still performed, because the brain is now working from habit, rather than the expectation of a reward.

Wendy Wood, PhD, a psychologist at The Habit Lab within the University of Southern California (USC), suggests that your daily habits occupy as much as 43% of your everyday actions whilst you are thinking about something else.

This automaticity is what makes habits so potent — they require less mental energy, enabling you to effortlessly integrate them into your daily routines.

Habits are the invisible architecture of our everyday lives.

Gretchen Rubin

Cracking the Habit Code — Unleashing the Power of Daily Habits

Your autopilot thrives on something popularly referred to as the habit loop. The term "habit loop" is a concept popularised in the field of behavioural psychology and habit formation studies. The habit loop, brought into mainstream literature by Charles Duhigg in his book "The Power of Habit: Why We Do What We Do in Life and Business," explains the neurological pattern that governs any habit, consisting of three components: the cue (or trigger), the response (or behaviour), and the reward. This was further expanded by James Clear in his book "Atomic Habits: An Easy & Proven Way to Build Good Habits & Break Bad Ones", who introduced a fourth element to the habit loop: craving. The strange thing is that it's not actually a loop, but a simple process flow.

When a cue appears, your autopilot initiates a response, aiming for the reward. For example, if you feel thirsty (cue), your body starts to want to drink (craving), which will prompt you to drink (response), resulting in the satiation of your thirst (reward). Over time, these behaviours become deeply ingrained. Understanding this process is akin to deciphering the ancient scripts of your own existence, allowing you to reprogram your autopilot by tweaking these habit flows to create a new neural pathway when you perform the response.

In today's world, this goes much further than physical behaviours and has us craving all manner of sensory and emotional experiences. From the desire to constantly check your smartphone, notification (cue) leading to a sense of anticipation and connection (craving), culminating in scrolling through social media (response), to the gratification of staying updated and entertained (reward). It looks a bit like this:

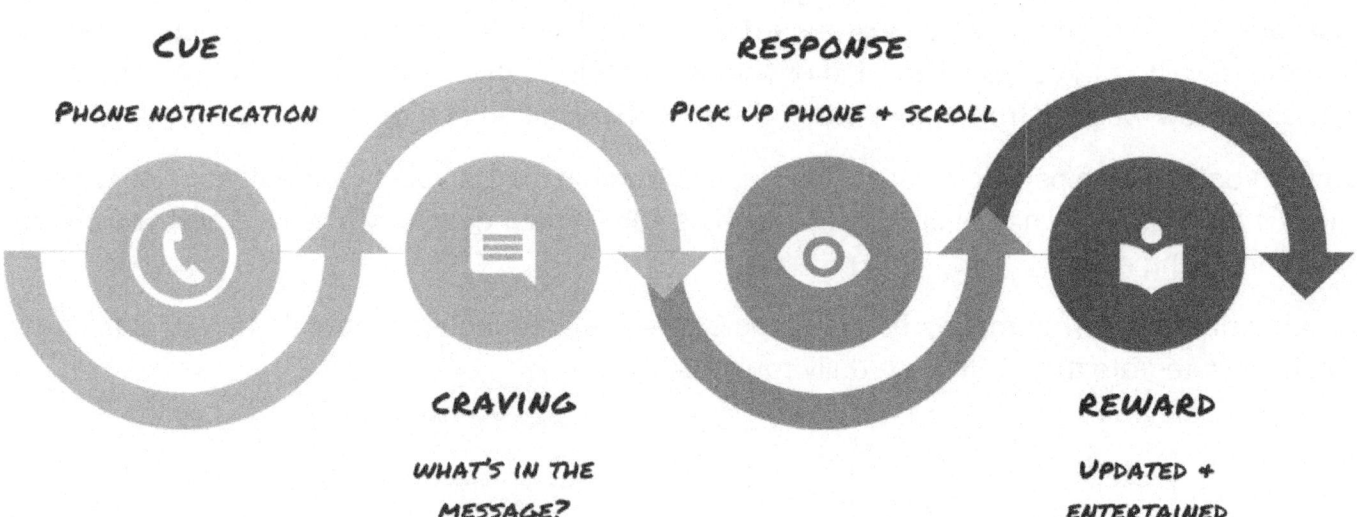

Similarly, the urge to indulge in sugary snacks (cue) can evoke a feeling of pleasure and excitement (craving), prompting us to consume the treat (response), ultimately resulting in the sweet taste and momentary bliss (reward). These habit flows are not limited to mere actions but extend to your thoughts and emotions, shaping your perceptions and responses in various situations.

This awareness grants you the power to reprogram your autopilot system by making subtle adjustments to your habit flows. By doing so, you can forge new neural pathways, fostering healthier responses and behaviours. This transformative process enables you to navigate the complexities of modern life, fostering mindfulness and intentional living amidst the constant barrage of sensory and emotional cues.

Changing a habit is never that simple. But by understanding the habit flow, we gain the power to change it.

The Cue

Every habit flow begins with a cue — a subtle nudge that prompts your brain to initiate a particular behaviour. Cues can be external, like the aroma of freshly brewed coffee in the morning, or internal, such as the gnawing feeling of stress. They act as signals, indicating it's time for your habit to commence. Cues are the catalysts, the initiators of habit formation. You already have a myriad of physical cues that exist with the habit loops that govern your bodily behaviours.

The first step in habit reformation is to identify a prompt or trigger event that initiates an interruption to your habit flow. By recognising these cues, you gain awareness of the patterns that lead to your habits. Awareness empowers choice. Once your psyche has been prompted to become aware of the need to pause, you can perform the new behaviour, whilst continuing with your existing response.

The Craving

The craving is the unsung hero of habit flows and the hidden force that drives your behaviour. It's the yearning, the desire, the insistent pull toward the completion of your response. Craving is the bridge between the cue and the response, the emotional charge that transforms a simple trigger into a powerful motivator.

In the context of Toothbrush Yoga, the focus lies in recognising these cravings exist and understanding the trigger events that interrupt the habit flow, paving the way for the integration of new yoga practices.

Cravings can manifest in various forms. It might be the anticipation of that first sip of coffee, the excitement of discovering a new post on social media, or the soothing comfort derived from indulging in a favourite snack. Cravings are deeply personal, influenced by your emotions, experiences, and desires, infusing your actions with purpose and urgency.

By deciphering these cravings, you can navigate your habit flows with insight and intention, ensuring that your responses align with your goals and aspirations. You can then learn to redefine your cravings, steering them toward habits that nurture your well-being and propel you toward your desired outcomes.

The Response

The response is the automatic sequence of actions you perform almost instinctively, often without conscious thought. For instance, the cue is smelling the coffee, and the response is buying and sipping the warm coffee, the cue is hearing the ping, and the routine is scrolling through social media. Or the cue is feeling a level of stress, and the response might be reaching for a comforting snack.

The Reward

Rewards are the linchpin holding the entire habit flow together. Rewards signify the brain's acknowledgement of a job well done.

Every response needs a reward — a shot of the feel-good chemical dopamine and a positive consequence that reinforces the behaviour and motivates repetition. Celebrating progress, no matter how minor, triggers the brain's reward centres, making the habit more appealing.

Rewards can be categorised into two main types: immediate rewards and delayed gratification rewards, otherwise known as incentives. Both techniques have their merits and can be used strategically to support your yoga practice.

Immediate Rewards

Consider dog training as an example. When you begin training a dog to come back or sit on command, you reward it with a treat for performing the behaviour. This is classified as an immediate reward, a satisfying, pleasurable outcome after completing the response.

If you gave the treat to the dog when you got home, there would be no way of associating the desired behaviour with the treat. Our brains work exactly the same.

An immediate reward is the most powerful because it associates the behaviour with the hit of dopamine. The reward is then used repetitively to reinforce the immediate behaviour, until such point, that the behaviour is ingrained, and the reward is no longer needed to achieve the behaviour.

The reward of a habit well-formed is a life well-lived.

Rewards play a more pivotal role than they seem at first glance. Whether it's rats, cats, dogs, chimps, or humans, numerous research papers demonstrate that behaviours can be modified through rewards. A reward, in the context of habit formation, isn't just a momentary pleasure or a fleeting indulgence, it's the fuel that propels your habit forward, reinforcing the neural pathways that make your new behaviour automatic, the glue that binds your behaviour to your brain.

Immediate rewards involve giving yourself a small, immediate treat or indulgence right after completing a yoga pose. These rewards provide instant pleasure and reinforce the positive experience of practicing yoga. They can range from a simple act of self-appreciation, like taking a moment to smile and acknowledge your effort, to treating yourself to a small piece of dark chocolate or a refreshing glass of water, to ticking off a completed task in your journal (more of that later). Immediate rewards create a sense of satisfaction, connecting the positive feeling with the completion of the pose. It's not the size of the reward that matters most; it's the sensation it evokes within you.

When you reward yourself after practicing Toothbrush Yoga, your brain will associate the positive experience with the specific routine, strengthening the neural pathways related to that habit. Over time, this reinforcement makes the habit more automatic and enjoyable. By acknowledging your efforts with rewards, you're nurturing the habit flow, ensuring that your commitment to Toothbrush Yoga becomes more ingrained and effortless.

Delayed Gratification/Incentives

Delayed gratification rewards take a different approach. Instead of providing an immediate reward, you hold off on the reward and only receive it after accomplishing a set of predetermined milestones or goals. For example, you may set a target of practicing yoga for a consecutive 30 days. Once you achieve this goal, you reward yourself with a more substantial treat, such as a spa day, a weekend getaway, or purchasing a new yoga accessory or outfit. It's important to note that as there is no dopamine release associated with the new behaviour, delayed gratification rewards don't have the power to neurologically impact your habits.

The benefit of delayed gratification rewards lies in the anticipation and motivation they build over time. By working towards the reward, you cultivate discipline and dedication to your yoga practice. The delayed gratification rewards act as a powerful incentive to stay committed to your routine and push through challenges. They reinforce the idea that the greatest rewards come to those who consistently put in the effort and show perseverance.

A reward is an immediate recognition of your practice, whereas an incentive is a future objective to motivate you to achieve something.

Which to Use and When?

When comparing immediate rewards and delayed gratification rewards, it's important to consider your personality and motivational preferences. Some individuals may find immediate rewards more effective, as they provide instant reinforcement and gratification, enhancing the immediate positive experience of practicing yoga. Others may be more motivated by delayed gratification rewards, as they appreciate the sense of accomplishment and the long-term benefits that come with reaching milestones.

Both techniques can be used in combination or alternated based on your preferences and desired outcomes. Experiment with different types of rewards to find what works best for you. The ultimate goal is to create a sustainable habit of practicing yoga, and the rewards you choose should align with that objective.

In conclusion, rewards are an integral part of reinforcing a habit stacking routine within Toothbrush Yoga. Immediate rewards offer instant gratification and enhance the positive experience, while delayed gratification rewards inspire discipline and long-term commitment. By understanding these techniques and tailoring them to suit your needs, you can create a powerful system of rewards that will support and strengthen your yoga practice for transformative results.

The Om Effect: Elevating Rewards Through the Ancient Power of Mantras

Probably not covered in any habit book ever, but using yogic mantras is worth considering as part of your reward system.

In yoga philosophy, the sacred syllable "Om" holds profound significance as the primordial sound from which all other sounds emanate. According to ancient beliefs, Om resounded at the inception of the universe, a cosmic resonance whose witness remains a mystery!

Within Hindu tradition, Om embodies the universal and original sound, while in Buddhism, it echoes as the sound of the universe itself. The Mandukya Upanishad, a revered yogic text, describes Om in expansive terms:

Om — This single syllable encapsulates the entirety of our world. Further elucidating, it signifies — the past, the present, the future — all encompassed in the resonance of Om.

Beyond its philosophical depth, Om holds a remarkable quality — it generates vibrations that resonate through the stomach and nose, inducing a calming effect on the nervous system. This harmonious sound contributes to stress reduction, lowering blood pressure and alleviating anxiety, making it a truly transformative and beneficial element in the practice of yoga and potentially the reward to your yoga practice.

It doesn't matter what the actual reward is, it's the act itself that counts, and if Om happens to work for you, all the better.

Mantras are the sacred melodies of the soul, guiding us towards deeper states of self-awareness through the practice of yoga.

Chapter 3: Hijacking the Habit Flow

When you think about adopting a healthier lifestyle, the idea of overhauling your entire routine to include regular yoga can be daunting. Committing the time to attend classes, comparing yourself to everyone in the room, not knowing how you should be doing a particular pose. I know, I've been there!

Toothbrush Yoga isn't about changing your lifestyle; it is designed to fit into your current routines, integrating yoga into pre-existing habits, in your own environment, without having to wear any Lycra, (although there is nothing to stop you if you want to!).

Habit is a cable; we weave a thread of it each day, and at last, we cannot break it.

Horace Mann

How is this possible? By pairing a new desired behaviour, (practicing a yoga pose), with a pre-existing ritual (for example flossing or showering). Something that routinely happens, consistently, on a day-to-day basis. This was first written about by BJ Fogg in his insightful book "Tiny Habits: The Small Changes that Change Everything". Fogg called this a habit recipe, which was then adopted by James Clear in his book Atomic Habits and renamed habit stacking. For this book, I will continue to refer to this as habit stacking. This process is also backed by extensive research, papers such as — The Importance of Creating Habits (American Journal of Medicine) and Routine and How are Habits Formed: Modelling Habit Formation in the Real World (European Journal of Social Psychology) — both of which provide great insight into how habit stacking can be leveraged for healthcare improvements in health. They're a bit of a dry read, but if you'd like some further insights, have a look through them, they're accessible in the Notes section in the Appendix.

The beauty of habit stacking lies in its ability to compound, or snowball into a significant transformation. It's not about the grand, sweeping changes that transform us overnight; it's about the small, consistent actions that accumulate over time.

Compound interest is the eighth wonder of the world. He who understands it earns it ... he who doesn't ... pays it

Unknown

Instead of having to go to a yoga class at 1900 every Monday and Wednesday, you simply integrate a yoga stretch into your morning ritual. At first, it might feel inconsequential, but over weeks and months, stacking incremental stretches to other routines. These daily stretches translate into improved elasticity, better posture, and enhanced vitality.

Consider for a moment how a task, performed for a small amount of time daily, can morph into a large number. If you performed a yoga pose for only 2 minutes whilst brushing your teeth each day, this will grow to 60 hours over 5 years, do this twice a day, and that's 120 hours.

DAILY	ONE MONTH	ONE YEAR	5 YEARS
2 MINUTES	1 HOUR	12 HOURS	60 HOURS
4 MINUTES	2 HOURS	24 HOURS	120 HOURS
10 MINUTES	5 HOURS	60 HOURS	300 HOURS
20 MINUTES	10 HOURS	120 HOURS	600 HOURS

This is the essence of the compound effect — the principle that states that even minor changes, when compounded over time, yield remarkable results.

Small Changes, Big Impact.

Every time you practice a Toothbrush Yoga pose in response to a cue, you reinforce these new neural pathways. With repetition, these pathways become stronger, gradually expanding your existing habits with new, healthier ones. These micro-adjustments accumulate over time, leading to significant progress without overwhelming challenges. With each repetition, you're nudging your autopilot toward a more mindful, healthier existence.

Life, as it turns out, is the sum of your small daily choices. This fundamental truth is the cornerstone of habit formation. A small, consistent effort, when repeated day after day, has the potential to balloon into significant, lasting change.

By embedding yoga poses within the fabric of your day, these micro-habits practiced consistently, become the foundation for a healthier lifestyle. When yoga becomes an integrated part of daily tasks, the physical, mental, and emotional benefits compound, leading to improved elasticity, better posture, enhanced focus, and reduced stress.

Beyond Routines: How Habit Stacking Amplifies the Power of Small

In order to attach a new habit to a pre-existing response, there must be an interruption to your autopilot mechanism. There needs to be a prompt to pause and allow the introduction of a new behaviour, stacked on top of the current one. Only by creating interruption to your autopilot, before you act upon the cue/craving, can you prevent the ingrained habit flow towards the response.

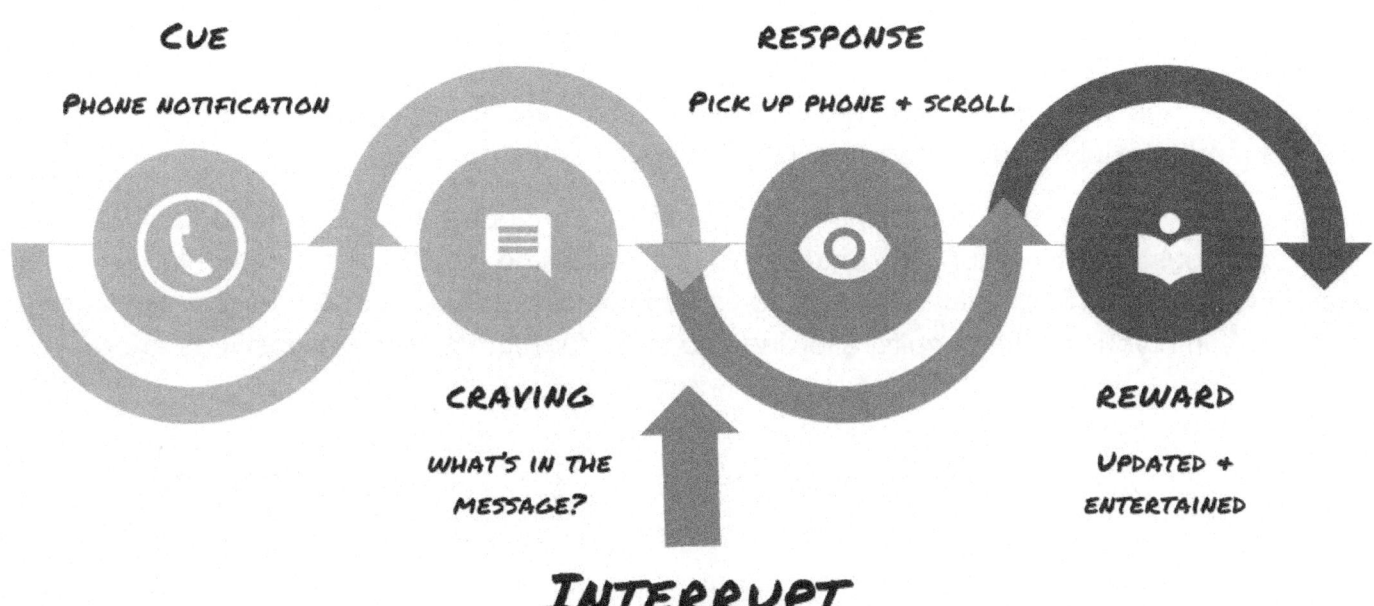

Once the interruption is recognised — I'll call this a habit prompt — a new operating response/habit (practicing a yoga pose) can be introduced into the habit flow. The habit prompt must be highly visible, something that can't be ignored and guaranteed to instigate the pause and allow you to initiate the new desired behaviour. By piggybacking the yoga pose onto the existing behaviour, a new habit flow is created.

With each habit stacked, your potential multiplies.

HABIT FLOW

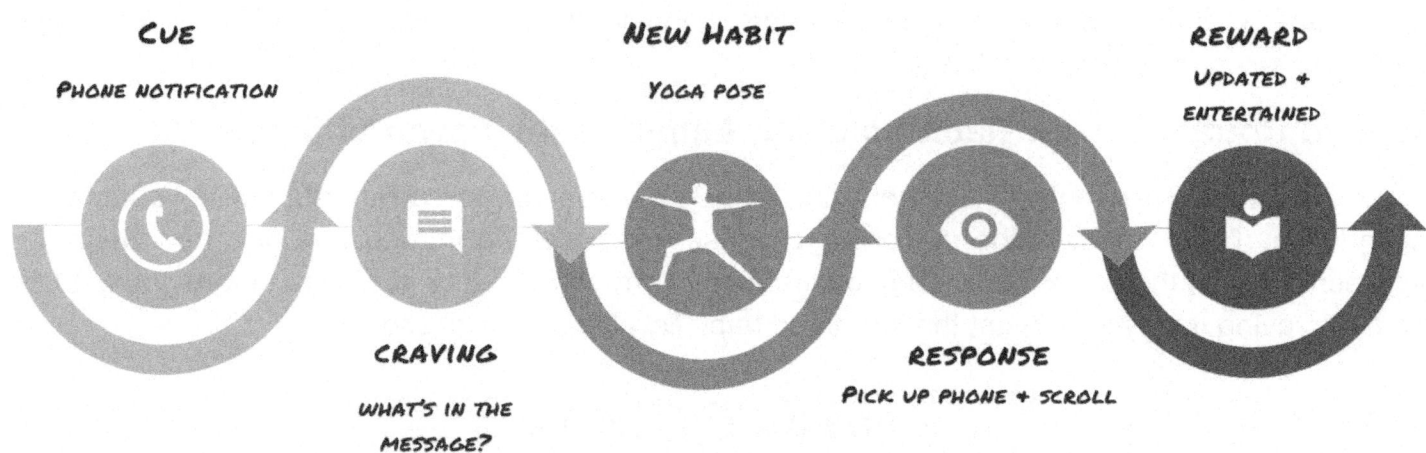

By identifying the cues that prompt your existing habits, and the craving that follows, understanding the routines they initiate, and acknowledging the rewards that follow, you gain profound insights into your behaviours. Armed with this knowledge, you can strategically modify your habits and embed yoga poses within your existing habit flows. It's easy when you know how!

The purpose of Toothbrush Yoga is therefore to reprogram your autopilot, to introduce yoga poses, initially consciously, within your daily rituals. As proven by the wealth of experiments conducted by researchers, this new habit stack will then evolve into your autopilot, unconsciously assimilating these new routines into your existing habits, allowing you to perform them without conscious effort.

Toothbrush Yoga becomes more than a habit-changing framework — it becomes a pathway to embodying the best version of you.

Let's Work Through a Toothbrush Yoga Example — Brushing your Teeth

I'm sure you can see that the research makes sense, but how do you do this in practice? Instead of striving for dramatic yoga milestones, in the beginning, the starting point needs to be small, incremental improvements. The key to building lasting habit stacking is to start with a small, easy task that takes between 30 seconds and two minutes to complete — mastering one pose at a time, refining your technique, and deepening your stretches gradually.

By doing so, you overcome the inertia of inaction and initiate the habit-building process. Your aim is to practice a Toothbrush Yoga pose within the context of your current response, for no more than two minutes. This is why toothbrushing is the ideal place to begin!

In this example, Toothbrush Yoga becomes an essential part of your daily toothbrushing ritual. The act of brushing your teeth serves as the cue, signalling the beginning of your Toothbrush Yoga practice.

Devoting a mere two minutes to this practice, both morning and evening, you effortlessly transform it into a lasting habit. The reward lies not just in the physical stretch but also in the mental tranquillity you've nurtured, enhancing your morning/bedtime ritual profoundly.

By making the task incredibly easy to start, you build momentum, increasing the likelihood of completing the task. Repetition is the key.

Cue: Identify the Prompt

- **Existing habit** — your daily toothbrushing ritual, a consistent moment of self-care twice a day.
- **Prompt** — place an elastic band, or some coloured tape around your toothbrush to act as the prompt. Whenever you pick up your toothbrush you will see and feel the elastic band, prompting you to practice your Toothbrush Yoga pose.

Craving: Recognise the Feeling

- **Desire** — the need to refresh your mouth and feel that minty just-cleaned taste when you get up or go to bed.

Response: Take Small, Consistent Actions

- **Consistent action** — every day, as you brush your teeth, practice a simple Toothbrush Yoga pose, such as the Forward Fold Pose, for two minutes while brushing your teeth. Feel the gentle stretch calming your body, harmonising with the rhythm of your breath.

Reward: Celebrate Progress and Success

- **Reward** — after completing the stretch, notice how your body feels, your legs, your glutes, etc. Smile! Tick off your daily stretch in your tracking app and notice a sense of accomplishment as you extend your streak further, reinforcing the habit flow positively.

Chapter 4: My Toothbrush Yoga Framework — Morning Ritual

Toothbrush Yoga offers a unique approach — you can integrate yoga poses seamlessly into your existing behaviours, modifying the cues, which in turn reminds you to perform an adjusted response. I can assure you this works, as I've done it.

I've been able to repeat these enough times to have forged new habit flows, effectively reprograming my autopilot to seamlessly integrate yoga into my pre-existing habits. By committing to daily habit changes, I've managed to create new habit flows, such that Toothbrush Yoga is now a natural part of my day.

Morning Ritual Habit Flow Map

Let's look at how this works in practice. Here is my morning — the flow of my morning rituals, starting with waking up through to finishing my breakfast. One routine leads to the next, to the next to the next. I pretty much perform this routine every day, regardless of where I am in the world. I don't think about it at all. It is my autopilot:

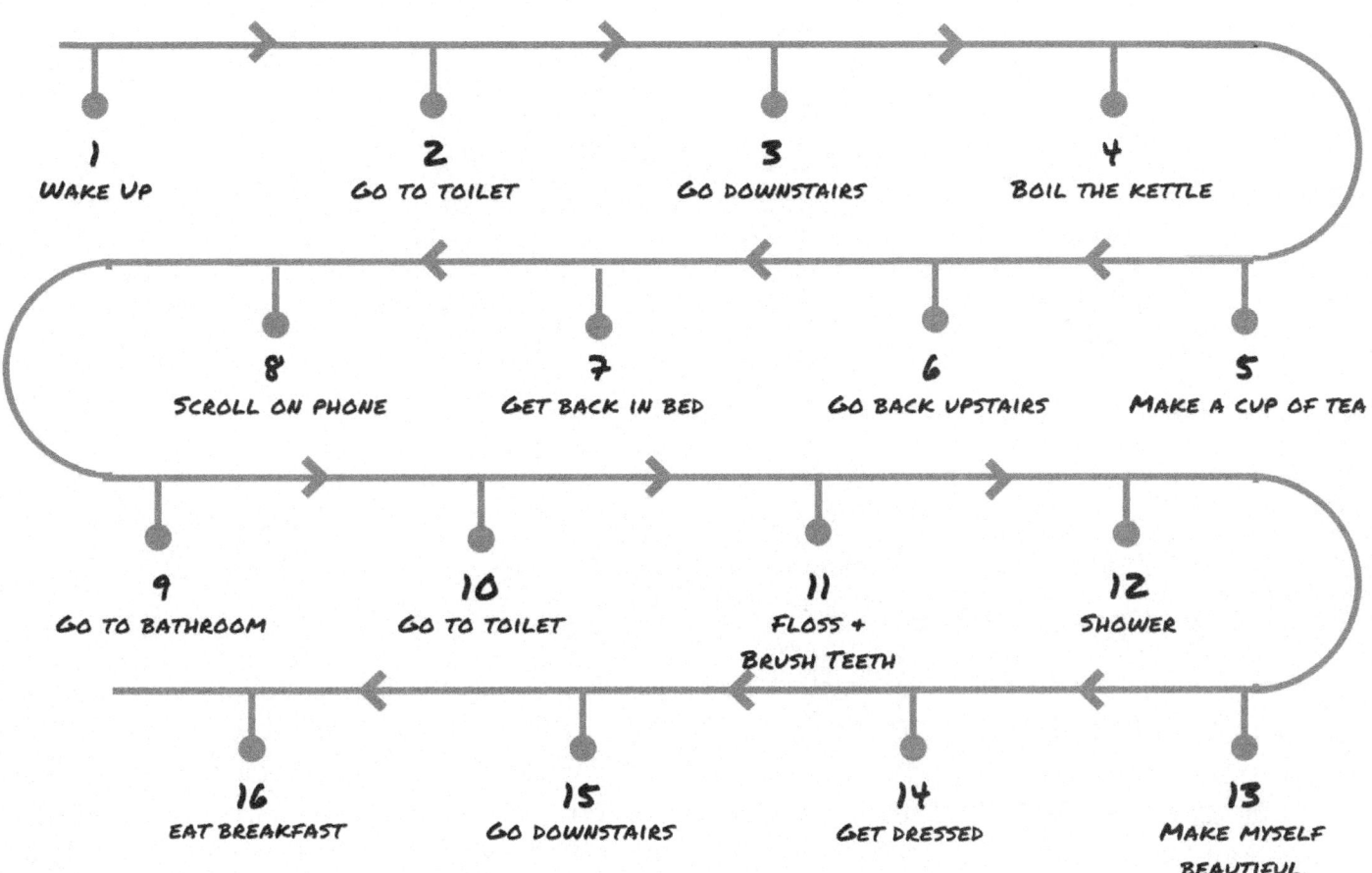

You may do some of these in a different order, such as brushing your teeth after eating breakfast, or maybe you skip breakfast altogether, however, I would imagine that your morning ritual is very similar.

There are nine habit flows, circled in the image below, on which I have stacked a Toothbrush Yoga pose. This is so well ingrained now that it requires zero conscious effort to perform. I'm like a well-trained dog, due to the repetition that I've performed over a long period. I need neither need the prompt, nor the reward to practice. It's a habit! Let me show you what habits I've chosen and which poses I've stacked on top of them.

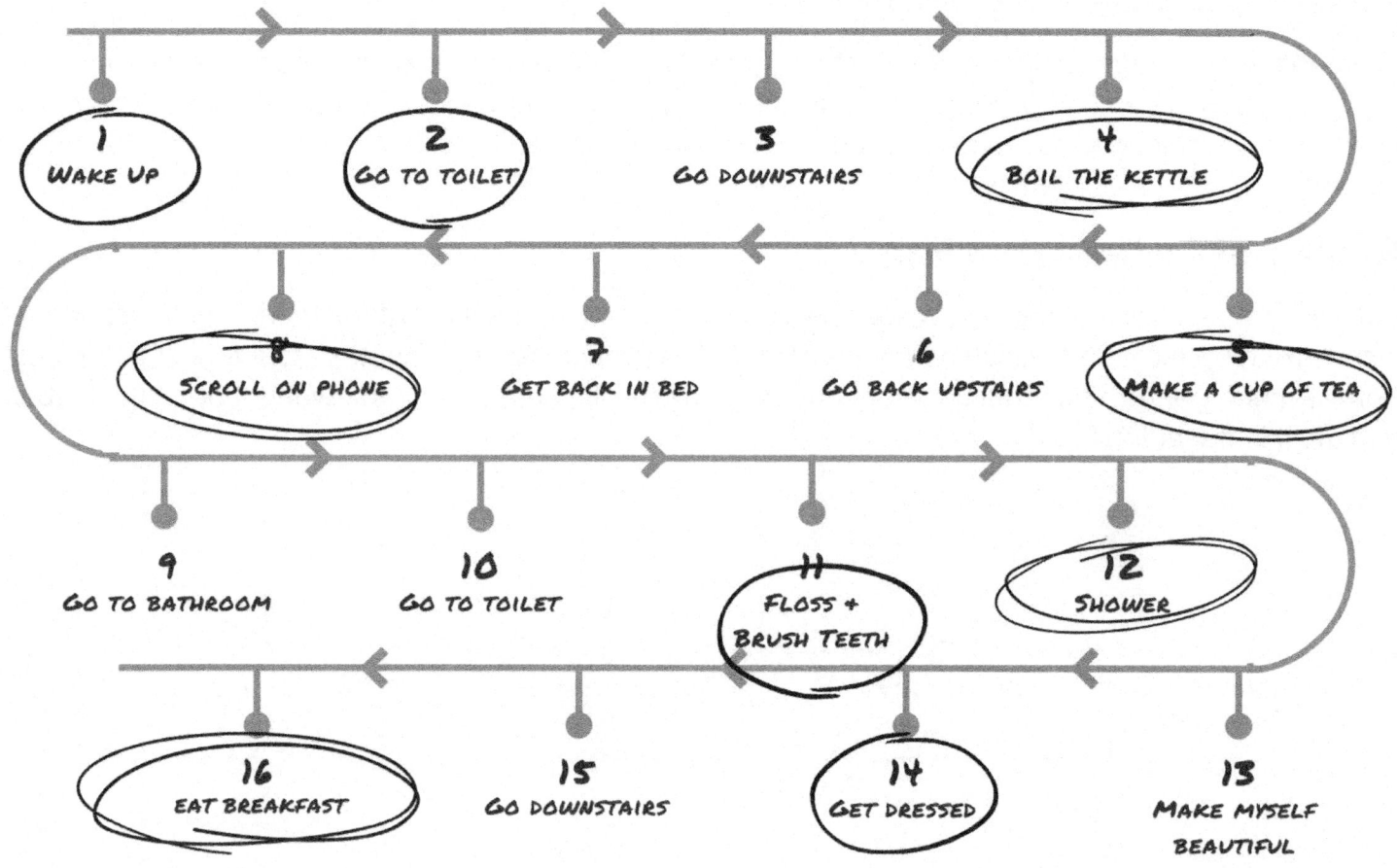

I'll run through each of these in turn, starting with waking up.

All of the poses mentioned are in the Toothbrush Yoga Pose Index later in the book, with pictures and a step-by-step guide so you can see how easy it is to do them! They are all pretty straightforward to do.

0630 — Wake Up — 5 Minutes

This is the easiest pose of all — a simple Corpse Pose, lying on my back and welcoming the day, centring my body and mind. Embrace this quiet moment, sync your breath with the subtle movements of a new day, and let your breath be your guide to a serene and mindful awakening. This is followed by a minute or two of Knees-to-Chest Pose or possibly turning over and coming into the Child's Pose for a gentle waking-up stretch. A lovely way to go from sleep to waking!

0640 — Go to the Toilet — 1 Minute

Standing at the toilet — I move into a heel-lifted Mountain Pose to bring balance to my body as I hold the pose.

Sitting on the toilet — a Seated Forward Fold Pose. Relaxing my lower back and hamstrings, for a gentle abdominal massage.

0645 — Boil the Kettle — 3 Minutes

Whilst I wait a few minutes for the kettle to boil, this is the perfect time to introduce a short Toothbrush Yoga practice.

Welcome to our kitchen! In the above sequence, I started in the Plank Pose, then transitioned into the Downward Dog Pose, followed by Triangle Pose and finally Extended Side Angle Pose. Just enough in the time it takes for the kettle to boil. All of these poses can be found in the section Toothbrush Yoga Pose Index.

You can adapt these poses and use any of the Standing Sequence Poses from the Index. I vary this sequence frequently to include Warrior 1 Pose, Warrior 2 Pose and Reverse Warrior Pose, remembering to practice this on both sides. You can either balance it out during the time the kettle takes to boil or do the other side of your body the next time you boil the kettle. Just be sure that you don't over-develop one side of your body. It's nice to be able to flow into different poses to help get the blood circulating for a bit of a wake-up.

0650 — Make a Cup of Tea/Coffee — 1 Minute

As I stand stirring the drink, this is the perfect time to hold a balance pose. Perhaps a few moments in the Tree Pose, remembering to balance on both right and left legs. Be mindful not to do this when holding a hot drink!

0655 — Return to Bed and Read/Use Phone — 5-15 Minutes

I will spend a little time here as I fully wake up and slowly (and carefully) take in my hot drink. I lie back on some pillows and move into the Reclining Bound Angle Pose or Frog Pose where I will stay for at least five minutes as I scroll through my phone and catch up with the day's news. As time passes the tension in my muscles slowly releases. After five minutes I vary my pose and move into Supine Spinal Twist, which I practice on both the left and right sides, again for five minutes each. For me, this is a great way to multi-task device time with well-being. After around 15 minutes I'm then ready to get up and I head into the bathroom.

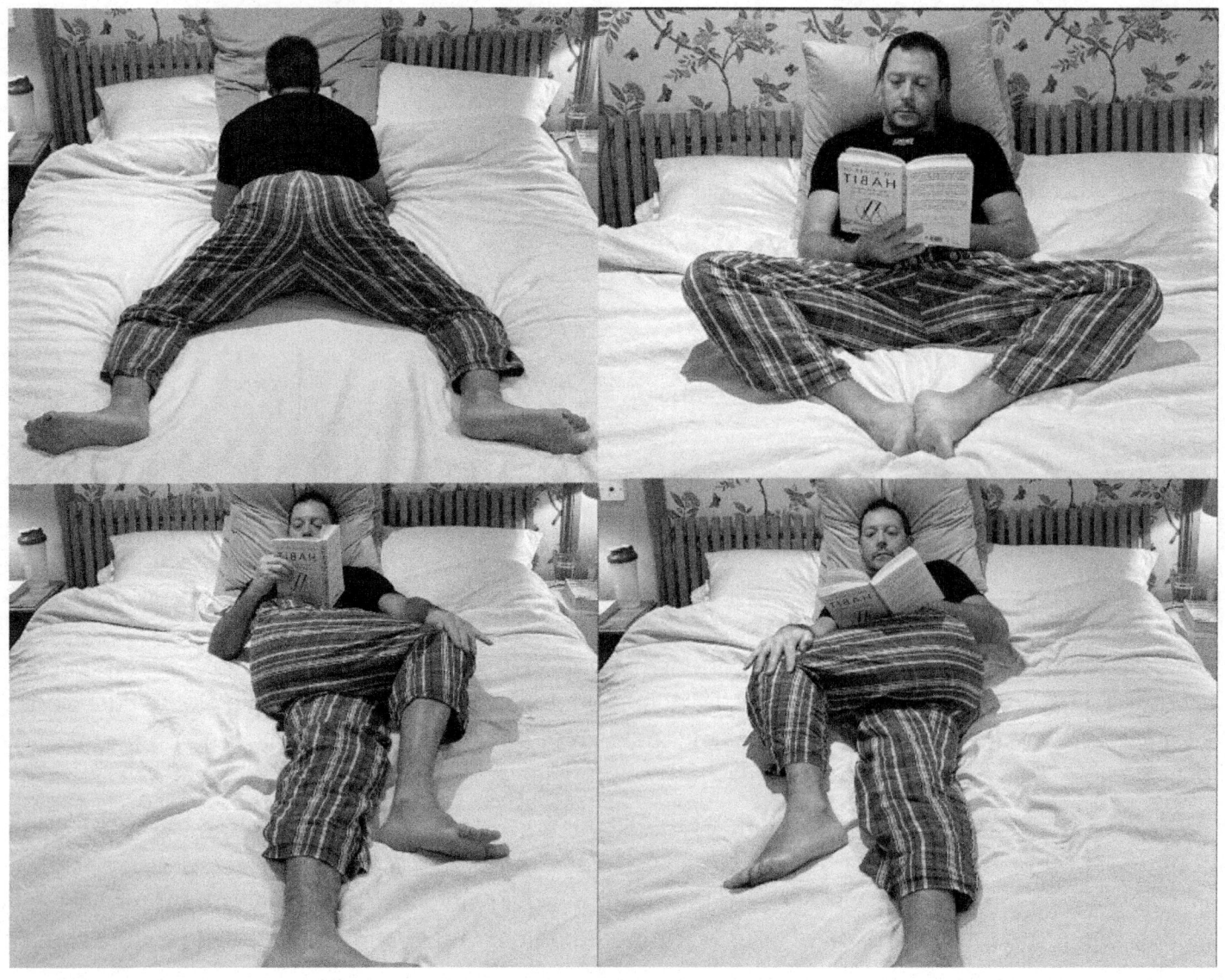

0710 — Floss and Brush Teeth — 3 Minutes

This is a great time to focus on Standing Poses. I practice a Forward Fold Pose followed by a Half Lift Pose after I've finished brushing my teeth. When I floss (I use a floss stick, rather than tape, so I only need one hand), I do one of the Standing Sequence Poses, in the photo I'm practicing the Dancer Pose. An easy way to multitask!

I don't just do this for the sake of it. Balance is hugely important for maintaining health in later life as it begins to diminish rapidly around the mid-fifties. The less stable we become, the more prone we are to falls, resulting in fractures as well as other health conditions.

A study in the British Journal of Sports Medicine discovered that the inability of middle-aged adults to stand on one leg for ten seconds was associated with a near doubling in the risk of death from any cause within the next 10 years!

The basic measure of balance is the duration for which you can stand on one leg, with your eyes closed. You're aiming for a minimum of 10 seconds. If this sounds easy, you need to try it. Despite being able to floss on one leg, whilst holding the other behind me, for about 2 minutes, I still struggle with closed-eyes balance. Given the research, I'm keen on improving this!

Withdrawal of the senses is like the consciousness entering the senses.

Yoga Sutra 2.54

0715 — Shower — 1 Minutes

Given the limited amount of room there is in my shower, I focus solely on Standing Balancing Poses. I opt for the Eagle Pose, as it's the only one that doesn't involve a leg poking out somewhere, and, depending on how awake I am, I might close my eyes as I lather up.

I don't recommend doing this until you've built up confidence in your balance on a dry surface. I also stop once I've got soap on the underside of my foot. Always prioritise your safety over the depth or intensity of any pose, especially on a wet/slippery surface!

0725 — Get Dressed — 1 Minute

I put my socks on whilst sitting on the bed where I complete a 30-second Seated Pigeon Pose on each side, whilst putting on my right and left socks. My goal is to touch my forehead against my shin. I can sometimes manage a nose touch, but I've still got a way to go here.

0735 — Eat Breakfast — 1 Minute

I'm generally sitting at the kitchen table eating breakfast, I'll practice a Seated Cat/Cow Pose. I can even do this if I'm eating with another person. It just looks like I'm stretching out the morning cobwebs (which I actually am), rather than practicing a Toothbrush Yoga pose.

0745 — Start the Day

There you have it, without changing into any yoga clothes, finding my mat, driving to a class, spending 45 minutes in a class, and then driving home, I've managed to generate a roughly 21-minute practice and all before my day has started.

Don't forget you can flex how many poses you do depending on your available time. Even just practicing a pose whilst you brush your teeth will yield significant benefits. If you are coming into this as a beginner, you should consider whether you need to modify the poses to make them attainable initially.

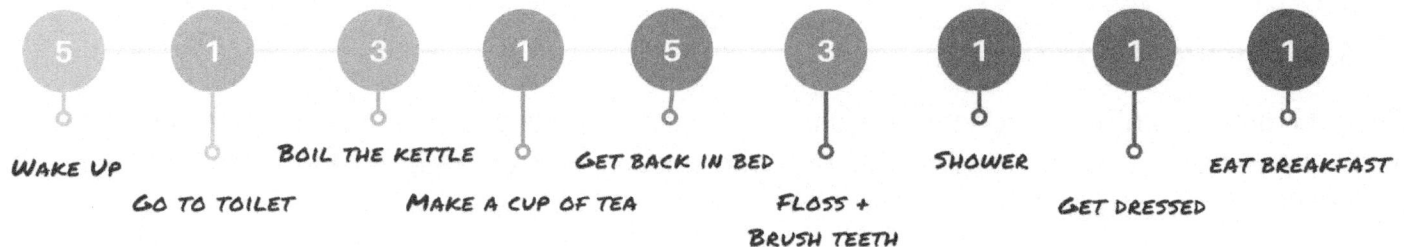

The table below provides a simplified view of what the poses look like, all of which can be found in the Toothbrush Yoga Pose Index.

Habit	Time	Pose	Position
Wake up	5	Corpse Pose, Knees-to-Chest Pose, followed by Child's Pose	
Go to the toilet	1	Mountain Pose on tip toes.	
Boil the kettle	3	Plank Pose, Downward Dog Pose, Triangle Pose, followed by an Extended Side Angle Pose	
Make a cup of tea	1	Tree Pose	
Scroll on Phone in Bed	5	Reclining Bound Angle Pose	
Floss and Brush teeth	3	Dancer Pose	
Shower	1	Eagle Pose	
Get dressed	1	Seated Pigeon Pose whilst putting on socks	
Eat Breakfast	1	Seated Cat/Cow Pose	

Rome Wasn't Built in a Day

My morning ritual developed over 3 months, beginning with a Forward Fold Pose whilst I brushed my teeth, from which I then stacked the other poses incrementally to my existing habits. I have to say you do look a little odd at first, but before you know it, it becomes a normal part of your day.

By seamlessly integrating yoga poses into your morning ritual, you will elevate your physical and mental well-being, ensuring a positive start to each day.

> *Each moment of your morning is an opportunity to connect with your body, mind, and spirit through the transformative power of yoga.*

Why not start your mornings with a wonderful sense of achievement to set you up for the day?

Hopefully, you can see how impactful this can be. There are several routines, like boiling the kettle, that are repeated throughout the day, so I also have the recall to repeat this time and again. The success of habit stacking hinges on selecting an appropriate anchor habit — it needs to be an existing routine that acts as a catalyst for your new habit, ideally occurring at the same time and in the same way, every day.

It would be no use choosing to practice a pose whilst I shaved for example, as I only do this once or twice a week, therefore the repetition would not be enough to successfully reprogram my neural pathways.

Build the Behaviour — Results Will Follow

The results of habit stacking are the natural by-product of consistent, mindful habits. When you focus on building the behaviour first, you're laying a foundation for a lifetime of wellness. Each yoga pose integrated into your day becomes a testament to your commitment to self-care and well-being.

> *It's not a race; it's a gradual, intentional journey.*

In the article — The New Rules of Stretching — published in the UK newspaper The Times, Tom Brownlee of the University of Birmingham was quoted "We need to work on our flexibility to maintain it and reap the benefits. Just a few minutes a day can make a difference. Start by stretching the body parts that give you the most discomfort, such as tight hips or hamstrings from sitting. The scientific consensus is that the benefits of functional movement and posture from daily stretching are seen within 4 weeks and after 16 weeks the gains are significant."

Additional Rituals for Habit Stacking

Beyond your morning rituals, we'll delve into various other routines you engage in throughout the next few chapters.

Chapter 5: Toothbrush Yoga at Work/Study

In today's fast-paced world, work and study will no doubt dominate your waking hours. According to the UK's Office for National Statistics, the average working week in the UK is 36.4 hours. That's a long time to be sitting at a desk or standing on your feet. The average working week is a substantial chunk of your productive hours in which there exists a wealth of opportunities to infuse mindfulness and yoga, enhancing both productivity and overall well-being.

These hours are littered with repetitive tasks, moments just waiting to be infused with mindful Toothbrush Yoga. Listed below are several suggestions where habit stacking opportunities exist.

Work-flow Wellness

- Attending meetings.
- Making phone calls.
- Conference calls.
- Reviewing and organising tasks.
- Completing assignments.
- Responding to emails and messages.

Mindful Pauses

- Drinks break.
- Snacking.
- Short walks or stretching breaks.
- Lunch break.
- Toilet breaks.
- Smoking breaks.

These will vary based on individuals' job roles, responsibilities, and workplace policies, but they provide a general overview of a typical working day.

Building a Mindful Work Environment — Finding the Right Prompt to Remind You

This is perhaps more challenging, depending on the work environment you're in. A shop worker will have a different set of prompts than that of a home worker, however, the challenges are the same. Here are some thoughts on what might work.

Setting the Tone — Arriving at Work

Placing a physical object on your coat hanger, desk, workstation, etc. can provide a physical cue to practice a quick stretching or breathing exercise.

Timely Reminders — Scheduled Moments

You could set a recurring private calendar reminder, an alarm or notification on your phone at a particular time, that will prompt you to practice the pose.

Hydration and Harmony — Drinks Break

Use a water bottle or coffee mug as a cue. This could have an elastic band on, a note, or a special message on the vessel. Every time you take a sip, maybe practice a seated yoga stretch or a neck rotation exercise.

Beyond the Smoke Screen

Smoking breaks are a prime candidate to Habit Stack a Toothbrush Yoga pose or two. It's better to stack against the cues of good habits, but we're just looking for any pre-existing habit to harness, even bad habits can have a side of goodness to them.

Even if you don't smoke, taking a smoking break is the perfect time to introduce stretch into your day. If you have a vape or a packet of cigarettes, place something on the item that you take with you and if you don't smoke, take a stress ball, or some kind of random object with you as your prompt. After all, why should smokers get to have all the breaks?

Every habit that you do is triggered by a cue, regardless of how subliminal it is to you. Smokers get an urge to smoke, or they are habituated by a time, place, or person. Latch on to these cues! You never know, you might just end up dropping your smoking habit for a yoga habit instead. ☺

By associating these cues/prompts with specific yoga practices, you can seamlessly integrate yoga into your work/study routines, enhancing both your physical and mental well-being.

There are only two mistakes one can make along the path of truth, not going all the way, and not starting at all.

Buddha

Chapter 6: Toothbrush Yoga in Everyday Tasks

Toothbrush Yoga extends far beyond the mornings and working hours; it seamlessly integrates into the countless other habitual tasks that your autopilot manages effortlessly. Whether you're washing dishes, cooking, doing laundry, driving, or even watching TV, these seemingly mundane chores can be transformed into valuable opportunities for mindful movement and holistic well-being. Let's run through some of them.

Yogic Fusion with Household Duties

Vacuuming — you might need a little invention to vary a pose(s) to suit how you practice this, but the Warrior poses can offer some excellent options. For instance, while vacuuming, you can incorporate a Crescent Lunge Pose or Warrior 2 Pose. This pose not only engages your legs and arms but also promotes focus and stamina, making it an ideal choice for a dynamic activity like vacuuming.

The cue could be getting the vacuum cleaner. Perhaps tie a knot in the cord so undoing this generates the prompt.

Any of the poses can be modified to suit your comfort and the nature of the task. This isn't a rigid structure, everything is adaptable. Listen to your body, maintain proper form, and enjoy the benefits of yoga even during your daily chores.

Yoga is not confined to the mat. It's about finding moments of peace and grounding, even while folding laundry or washing dishes.

Washing dishes — this is the perfect time to practice a standing balance pose, a Tree Pose (see photo), or maybe even a variation of Warrior 3 Pose (see the Toothbrush Yoga Pose Index, as you'll need your hands available). The cue might be to place your washing-up liquid in a different or hard-to-reach place.

Hanging out the washing — a Chair Pose is ideal for squatting down, picking up the clothes, standing and placing them on the clothesline. Your cue could be storing the clothes pegs in a different location.

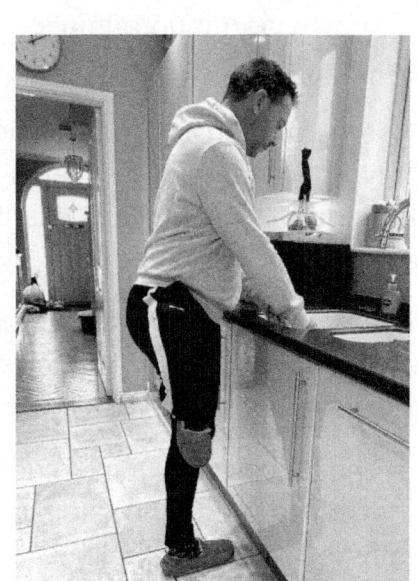

Travelling/Commuting — Stop Means Start

Driving or taking public transport are ideal moments to introduce a mindful pose. When you're stuck at traffic lights, you can use those moments to practice yoga and promote relaxation. Here are a few poses that can be practiced inside the car/bus while it is stationary: Seated Cat/Cow Pose, Seated Side Twist Pose, Seated Side Bend Pose or a partial Seated Forward Fold Pose.

Always prioritise safety when practicing yoga in the car! Keep your attention on the road and only practice poses when the vehicle is stationary, ensuring you can always maintain full control of the vehicle.

When standing on public transport, incorporate balancing poses into your journey — they can be a highly effective way to strengthen your body. The swaying motion of the vehicle naturally engages your muscles, requiring them to contract and counterbalance your movements and leading to increased strength, especially in your back region.

Cues for the car could be a Post-it note on your dashboard, while travelling on public transport this could be the feeling of the vehicle's movement. Each time you sense the swaying or rocking motion of the transport, let it serve as a reminder to engage in a balancing yoga pose.

Find stillness amidst the chaos. Let the traffic of thoughts pass by as you navigate the highways of life.

Yoga isn't just about poses - intentional breathing in stressful circumstances such as driving or on public transport, can have a hugely positive effect. Deep breathing exercises such as belly breathing, also known as diaphragmatic breathing, can be incredibly calming, activating the parasympathetic nervous system.

Belly breathing involves breathing deeply into the abdomen, allowing the diaphragm to fully expand. This type of breathing activates the body's relaxation response, reducing stress and anxiety levels. It also triggers the release of calming neurotransmitters, promoting a sense of peace and tranquillity. As a result, this deep breath can slow down the heart rate, also helping to reduce blood pressure.

A research paper on "The physiological effects of slow breathing in the healthy human", published in the National Library of Medicine, uncovered significant effects of belly breathing on the respiratory, cardiovascular, cardiorespiratory, and autonomic nervous systems.

This can encourage mindfulness during your journey, relieving the stress caused by commuting. Guidance on breathing exercises can be found in the Developing Toothbrush Yoga Further — The Breath as Life Force section.

Standing Strong — Embracing the Power of Balance in Ordinary Moments

Standing in line at the grocery store, waiting for public transport, or queuing up anywhere offers an excellent opportunity to practice a standing balance pose. I'm not suggesting you contort into a full Eagle Pose and wrap your arms and legs around each other and squat and the supermarket! Instead, simply transition into the Mountain Pose and find your balance on your toes or shift your weight onto one leg at a time. Engage in subtle movements while maintaining a conscious breath.

During these moments, you can attach any mental or physical cue to this practice. As frustration builds in the situation, let that feeling be the trigger that prompts you to embrace this pause positively, utilising it as an opportunity to bring Toothbrush Yoga into your day (as well as relaxing you and reducing stress as a reward!).

Pausing with Purpose — Embracing Tranquillity

In your daily life, there will be moments to pause, unwind, and engage in leisure activities. Whether you're scrolling through your phone, watching TV, or reading a book, these instances offer an ideal opportunity to introduce relaxation through Toothbrush Yoga. Here are some cues and Toothbrush Yoga poses ideal for these tranquil moments.

Balancing Tech and Health — Blending Device Usage with Yogic Poses

You might spend too much time on your devices. Just imagine how much benefit you could gain if, whilst you were scrolling through social media, or reading the latest sports bulletin you were engaged in an activity that was physically benefiting you at the same time.

To make the most of your screen time, the establishment of a cue that prompts the impulse to practice a yoga pose each time you pick up your phone or tablet is crucial.

You might have a screen saver, a phone case message, a sticker, maybe place your phone away from you once you've looked at it, turn off the fingerprint, or facial recognition, so you must type in your passcode, 96428463 spells out yogatime, which will trigger the recall. Whatever you decide upon, it needs to be obvious.

Once you have the cue, depending on whether you are standing, seated, or lying down, there are numerous poses that you can practice.

- **Standing with your device** — any of the balance poses or perhaps a Forward Fold Pose or Half Lift Pose.
- **Sitting with your device** — Seated Pigeon Pose.
- **Lying with your device** — for an amazing stretch, there is nothing better than the Reclining Bound Angle Pose. You can stay in the position for 5 minutes at a time, as with Supine Spinal Twist. Don't forget to practice on both the left and right sides. Legs Up the Wall Pose is a great one for just chilling out, either with or without the wall or Boat Pose which will need to be modified a little as you'll have your device in your hands. Lift those legs and let your six-pack develop as you happily scroll through your device. By associating these poses with your device usage, you'll seamlessly incorporate yoga into your screen time, making it a physically enriching experience.

Zenful Viewing — The Power of Pause: Enhancing TV Time with Mindful Movement

As you settle in front of the TV, commercial breaks provide the perfect cues to trigger your Toothbrush Yoga habit. Each break gives you a few minutes to disengage from the programme and adopt whatever pose suits your environment. For example, Boat Pose and Knees-to-Chest Pose are both great choices to try for a few minutes, particularly as they're symmetrical, so you don't need to practice on both sides.

Once the action restarts, you can either drop the pose or move into some of the poses suggested in the previous Zenful Viewing — The Power of Pause: Enhancing TV Time with Mindful Movement section and carry on whilst you absorb the programme.

Let yoga be your companion as you binge-watch your favourite TV show, reminding you to relax and find joy in downtime.

From Words to Wellness

There is no better time than when you pick up a book to engage in a little mindful Toothbrush Yoga. Your cue could be as simple as a bookmark with a message on it. Every time you open the pages to read, you're confronted with an obvious prompt.

Your location/physical position will dictate which poses are suitable, but there are a couple of poses perfect for reading. When sitting the Easy Seating Pose and Reclining Bound Angle Pose are good; for more supple practitioners the Half Lotus Pose is a great option. Introducing a mindful breath exercise would also enhance this for you.

Chapter 7: Toothbrush Yoga in Evening Rituals

Much like your morning habits, your evening ritual will also be steeped in a series of repetitive tasks, each one leading you closer to the moment you slip into the realm of dreams.

Introducing Toothbrush Yoga into your evening rituals can aid in relaxing both your body and mind, creating a soothing bedtime, grounded in yoga and mindfulness. These habitual tasks provide the perfect moments for integrating Toothbrush Yoga, fostering a profound sense of relaxation and serenity, paving the way for a peaceful and restful sleep. Let's explore some common evening routines and how you can infuse them with yoga and mindfulness.

The Power of Bedtime Rituals

As you saw from the morning rituals, you will have a defined set of activities such as going to the toilet, brushing your teeth and skincare regimes, all leading up to you finally sliding into bed. Each one of these moments, as before, presents an opportunity to habit stack, associating a Toothbrush Yoga pose with each routine.

Many of these activities mirror what you do in the morning. Perhaps you can attach the same Toothbrush Yoga pose in the morning *and* the evening to reinforce the habit? After all, it's the repetition of the habit, not the duration that matters. Let's remind ourselves of some of the poses you can do with each habit:

Habit	Pose	Position
Going to the toilet (seated)	Seated Side Twist Pose or Seated Forward Fold Pose	
Brushing your teeth	Low Lunge Pose	
Taking of your make up	Tree Pose	

The practice of yoga before bed has the power to transform restlessness into serenity, fatigue into relaxation, and chaos into calm.

Cultivating Relaxation — Getting Ready for Bed

As you settle into bed, you will no doubt undertake a series of small habits, like closing the blinds, filling a glass of water, reaching for the eye mask, picking up a book to read, and plugging in your phone. Each of these habits can have a Toothbrush Yoga pose stacked onto them.

What cues can you put in place to prompt you to do this? Your blinds might have a tag on the cord that pulls them shut, your water glass could have a sticker, your eye mask might be placed in a bag from when you woke up, and your book has a bookmark in it. All of these cues can lead you to practice a pose in those moments, a Downward Dog Pose after closing the blinds, a Seated Side Twist Pose when you sit on the bed, or a Locust Pose when you pull back the covers on the bed.

The beauty of incorporating yoga poses into your evening rituals is that not only will they enhance your physical adaptability, but they also nurture mental tranquillity.

As a final signal before sleep, perhaps stretch and elongate your body, whilst engaging in deep, calming breaths. This will enable you to embrace the stillness of the moment and cultivate a serene atmosphere before sleep.

Yoga relaxes your nervous system and reduces stress, fostering better sleep.

Before you finally slip off into unconscious dreaming, take your last pose, Corpse Pose. This is one of the most important and beneficial yoga poses. Despite its seemingly simple nature, Corpse Pose is a powerful practice for deep relaxation and rejuvenation with the primary intention of the pose to bring complete relaxation to the body, mind, and spirit. It's a moment of surrender, allowing practitioners to let go of physical and mental tension, promoting a sense of calm and inner peace.

Incorporating Corpse Pose into your yoga practice provides a profound opportunity for relaxation and self-discovery. It serves as a reminder of the importance of embracing stillness and tranquillity in your often hectic life, allowing you to gently drift off to sleep.

Corpse Pose isn't merely a physical posture; it's a sanctuary of the mind, a time to release the tensions of the day, both physical and mental, and to prepare your being for a restful night's sleep.

In this quietude, you have the opportunity to engage in visualisation — a powerful technique that transcends the boundaries of the physical body. Close your eyes and let your imagination take flight. Picture yourself in a place of utter tranquillity, perhaps a serene beach at sunset, a lush forest, or a field of blooming flowers. Feel the gentle caress of the breeze, hear the soothing sounds of nature, and immerse yourself in a scene of pure bliss.

As you visualise this peaceful environment, let go of any lingering thoughts or concerns from the day. Allow your mind to wander freely, embracing the beauty of the present moment. With each breath, imagine inhaling positivity and exhaling any remaining tension or worry. Visualise your body becoming weightless as if you're floating on air, unburdened by the stresses of the day.

Savasana and visualisation together create a sacred space for you to bid farewell to the day, acknowledging its challenges and triumphs while embracing a sense of inner calm. As you slowly transition from this tranquil state to prepare for sleep, carry this serenity with you, allowing it to permeate your dreams and nurture your subconscious mind. Through Savasana and visualisation, you conclude your day with a harmonious balance of relaxation and mindfulness, paving the way for a peaceful night and a rejuvenated tomorrow.

The body benefits from movement, and the mind benefits from stillness.

Sakyong Mipham

Notes

Chapter 8: Your Toothbrush Yoga Framework

This chapter empowers you to create your own personalised Toothbrush Yoga framework. I'll navigate you through the 10-step process, starting with your desired outcomes, the identity you will adopt, the what, the where, the when and the how of your Toothbrush Yoga intentions, and finally the goals that you want to set yourself. The simple approach of planning out these details increases your chances of getting started and following through as proven in Mindset Theory of Action Phases published in the Encyclopedia of Personality and Individual Differences.

Toothbrush Yoga Framework Pyramid

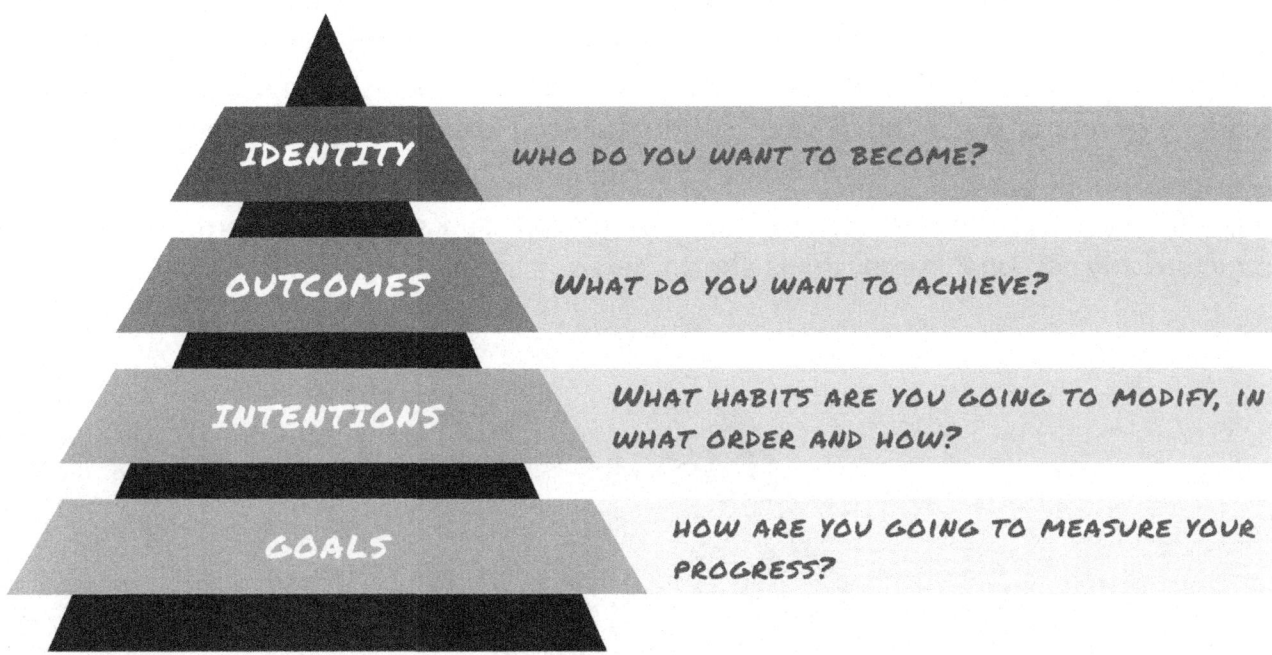

Identity is your compass, outcomes set the course, intentions fuel the journey and goals demark the milestones. You guide the expedition.

Structuring Your Yoga Journal

It's at this point that I want you to visualise and document your approach to Toothbrush Yoga. Through the act of writing, you bring your intentions and desires into focus, therefore it's time to dig out that new notebook I mentioned previously. You can of course do this online too. Whatever works best for you. I have provided pre-formatted templates, which can be downloaded for free and are available in the Free Bonus Content section within the Appendix when you sign up for the Toothbrush Yoga Newsletter. The following headings can help you record how you intend to implement and measure your progress:

- **Identity and beliefs** — reflect on the person you are becoming through your yoga practice. What beliefs are shaping your identity as a Toothbrush Yogi? Acknowledge the positive shifts in your mindset and self-perception.
- **Outcomes** — begin your journal by articulating your desired outcomes. What are you aiming to achieve with Toothbrush Yoga? Whether it's enhanced suppleness, inner peace, or better posture, reaffirm your objectives to anchor your practice.
- **Morning, Work/Study, Everyday, and Evening Ritual Intentions** — then, set out your habit flows and intentions for the rituals you have identified and define the ranking, poses, prompts, and rewards.
- **Long-term goals** — next consider where you want to be in the course of the following 3, 6 and 12 months? Where do you want to be thereafter?
- **Short-term goals** — finally, define how you want to track your progress with your goals. Setting clear goals gives your practice direction and purpose. It could be the depth of stretch, the frequency of your practice, the duration of your balance, or how long it took you to go to sleep.

Each of the elements within the Toothbrush Yoga framework cascades downwards building a solid pyramid structure. My personal framework is shown below.

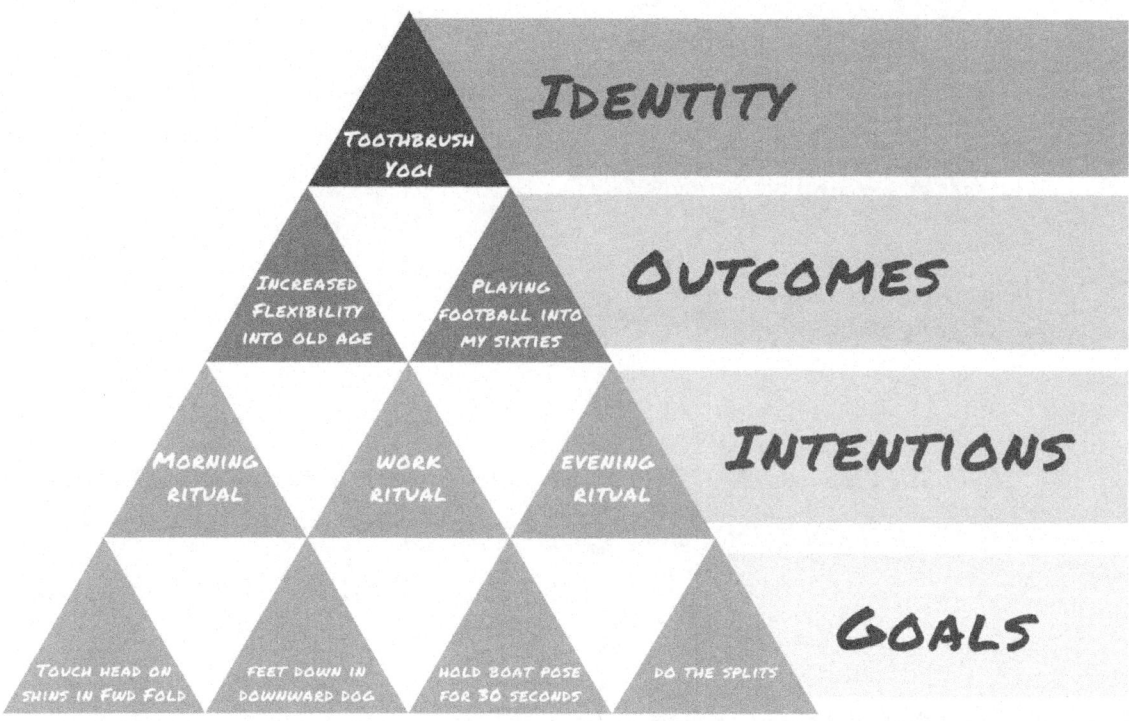

I'm now going to help you to create your own framework. I want you just to read through the 10 steps in the coming pages to help you understand and begin to visualise *your* approach to Toothbrush Yoga. Have your notebook to hand and jot down any ideas that spring to mind initially so you don't lose them, maybe create a mind map as you read through this chapter.

I then want you to come back to the start of this chapter and begin to work through and document your approach. Through the act of writing, you bring your intentions and desires into focus.

STEP 1 — Setting Your Course — Your Desired Outcomes

Whilst Identity sits at the top of the framework pyramid, it's easier to start building out your framework by reflecting on your deepest desires. What aspects of your physical and mental well-being would you like to enhance? Is it increased elasticity, improved posture, reduced stress, or improved overall fitness? Your outcomes should resonate with your core desires, inspiring you every time you think about it. It's far easier to initially think about what you want to achieve before who you want to become.

Think about the long-term impact of your outcomes. How will increased flexibility or reduced stress benefit your overall well-being? Consider the positive effects on your daily life, relationships, and overall happiness. Envision the transformative power of your outcomes, anchoring it in the broader context of your life's aspirations.

Your outcomes should align with your core values. If you value holistic health, one outcome might involve enhancing both physical and mental well-being. If you value self-discovery, another outcome might focus on exploring your body's capabilities and pushing your boundaries. If you want to use this process to develop your spiritual side, you might want to deepen the connection between your body and mind. Aligning your outcomes with your values creates a profound sense of purpose and authenticity.

Try closing your eyes and visualising your future self, embodying your desired outcomes.

How does it feel to move with grace and limberness? What does reduced stress look like in your posture and facial expressions? Visualisation creates a vivid mental image, making your outcomes tangible and inspiring. Use this visualisation to fuel your motivation and dedication.

Take the time to reflect, visualise, and align your outcomes with your values, and let it become the guiding light illuminating your path to self-discovery and empowerment.

Sometimes it is hard to distil your outcomes into something tangible without writing it down. I suggest jotting down a mind map, word cloud, or creating a mood board to help you clarify your thoughts.

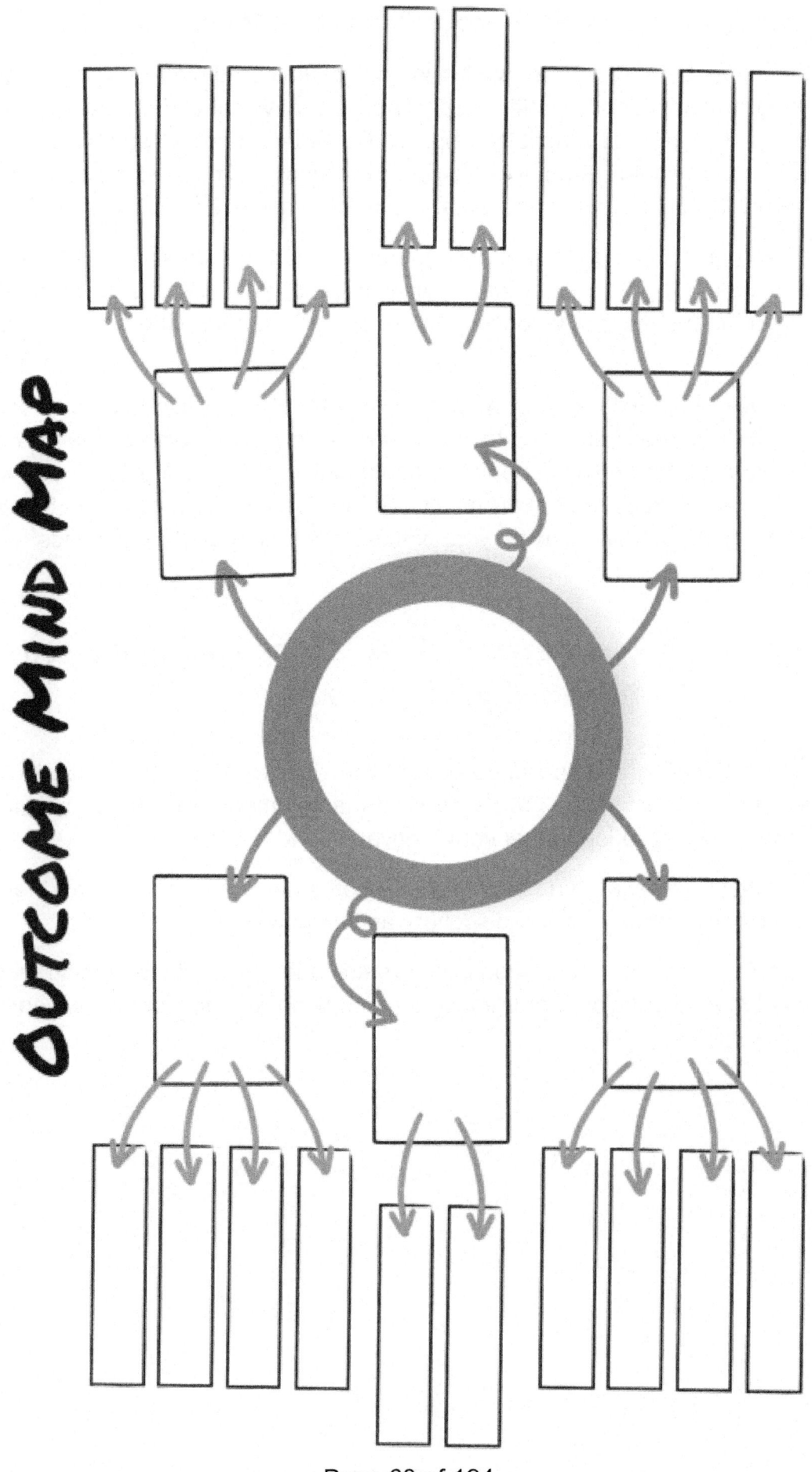

STEP 2 — Navigating Your Path — Identity and Beliefs

Now you have considered the outcomes you want to achieve, it's time to reflect on who you need to become to reach them. Defining your identity within the context of Toothbrush Yoga is a profound exploration of self. It's not merely about who you are now; it's about becoming the best version of yourself and aligning your beliefs, values, and habits with this ideal identity.

> *Our habits shape our identity, for it is through consistent action that we become who we aspire to be.*

What follows is a deeper exploration of how to determine who you want to become:

Begin by engaging in self-reflection. Identify your core values — those fundamental principles that guide your life. Your identity should align seamlessly with these values. If authenticity, health, or resilience are central to your values, your Toothbrush Yoga identity should reflect these principles.

Envision your aspirational self — the person you aspire to become. What qualities does this future version of yourself possess? Is it confidence, discipline, inner peace, or physical strength? Your identity should encapsulate these qualities, serving as a beacon guiding your actions and choices.

Your identity is shaped by your beliefs about yourself. Identify and embrace positive beliefs that empower your journey. Replace self-limiting beliefs with affirming statements. For example, replace "I'm not flexible" with "I am becoming more flexible every day." Positive beliefs reinforce your identity, fostering self-confidence and determination.

Again, I strongly encourage you to write down what you see as your future identity as well as some positive mantras or intentions. Add them to your journaling notebook. Perhaps also write a mantra down on a colourful Post-it and leave it on your bathroom mirror as a positive reminder of who you want to be and the outcomes you are seeking. I connect with the following mantras:

- I am open to learning new things.
- I don't need to be perfect.
- I am enough.
- I do not compare myself to others.
- My mind is relaxed and clear.
- I am creative.

Remember that your identity is not fixed; it will evolve as you grow and learn. Engage in continuous self-discovery. Be open to exploring new facets of yourself and embracing evolving identities. Embracing change and growth is inherent to your Toothbrush Yoga identity.

Defining your identity within the Toothbrush Yoga framework is a transformative and empowering process. It's about becoming the best version of yourself — one Toothbrush Yoga practice at a time. Embrace your core values, passions, and positive beliefs, align them with your goals, and let this authentic identity guide your Toothbrush Yoga journey toward holistic well-being and self-discovery.

STEP 3 — Fuelling the Journey — Your Toothbrush Yoga Intentions

It could be as uncomplicated as starting with incorporating a Forward Fold Pose whilst you brush your teeth. Starting small eliminates the overwhelming feeling of change and allows you to establish a foundation.

The journey towards integrating yoga into your daily routine doesn't require a drastic overhaul of your life. In fact, it begins with a single, manageable habit.

Imagine beginning your day with a single yoga pose, say the rejuvenating Cat/Cow Pose. Over the course of a week, this one-minute practice becomes a familiar friend. You wake up, before you pick up your phone, without much thought, you assume the Cat/Cow position. The key here is consistency. By consistently practicing this one pose, it becomes ingrained in your morning ritual, a new habit is formed.

Toothbrush Yoga habit formation is akin to sculpting the mind and body through gentle, persistent practice. It's a transformative journey where consistent actions reshape the neural landscape of your brain. As you repeat your Toothbrush Yoga poses and mindfulness exercises, your brain undergoes a remarkable process called long-term potentiation. This intricate mechanism strengthens the connections between neurons, optimising your brain's efficiency in performing these activities. This phenomenon is affectionately referred to as "Yogic Synapses," where each repetition deepens the cellular conversations, enhancing the harmony between your body and mind.

This concept echoes the wisdom of Hebb's Law, "neurons that fire together wire together". The simultaneous activation of nearby neurons leads to an increase in the strength of the synaptic connection between them, encapsulating the essence of Toothbrush Yoga: the unity of neural firing and mindful wiring, creates the foundation for not just enduring habits, but mindfully beneficial habits.

Personalised Blueprint — Mapping out Your Rituals/Routines

It's time to define how you will take your Toothbrush Yoga intentions forward and define your plan of what, where, when and how you will incorporate Toothbrush Yoga into your day-to-day life. Only you know yourself best and can determine whether you want to focus on your Mornings, Work/Study, Everyday or Evening Rituals or a combination of them all. By setting this out in writing you create your own system of accountability. Just remember the study published in The British Journal of Health Psychology, which found that 91% of participants who defined their intention to exercise by writing down when and where they would exercise ended up following through. Let me be clear on this last point:

WRITE IT DOWN!!!

What Does Your Morning Ritual Look Like? — Define Your Habit Flow Map

Let's start this process by mapping out your Morning Rituals. Using my example in Chapter 4: My Toothbrush Yoga Framework — Morning Ritual as a guide, map out the sequence of events/tasks from waking up through to when you are ready to start your day, 1 leads to 2 leads to 3, etc. Below is a blank Habit Flow Map. There are also several pre-formatted templates, including a blank Habit Flow Map Template, which can be downloaded for free and is available in the Free Bonus Content section within the Appendix when you sign up for the Toothbrush Yoga newsletter.

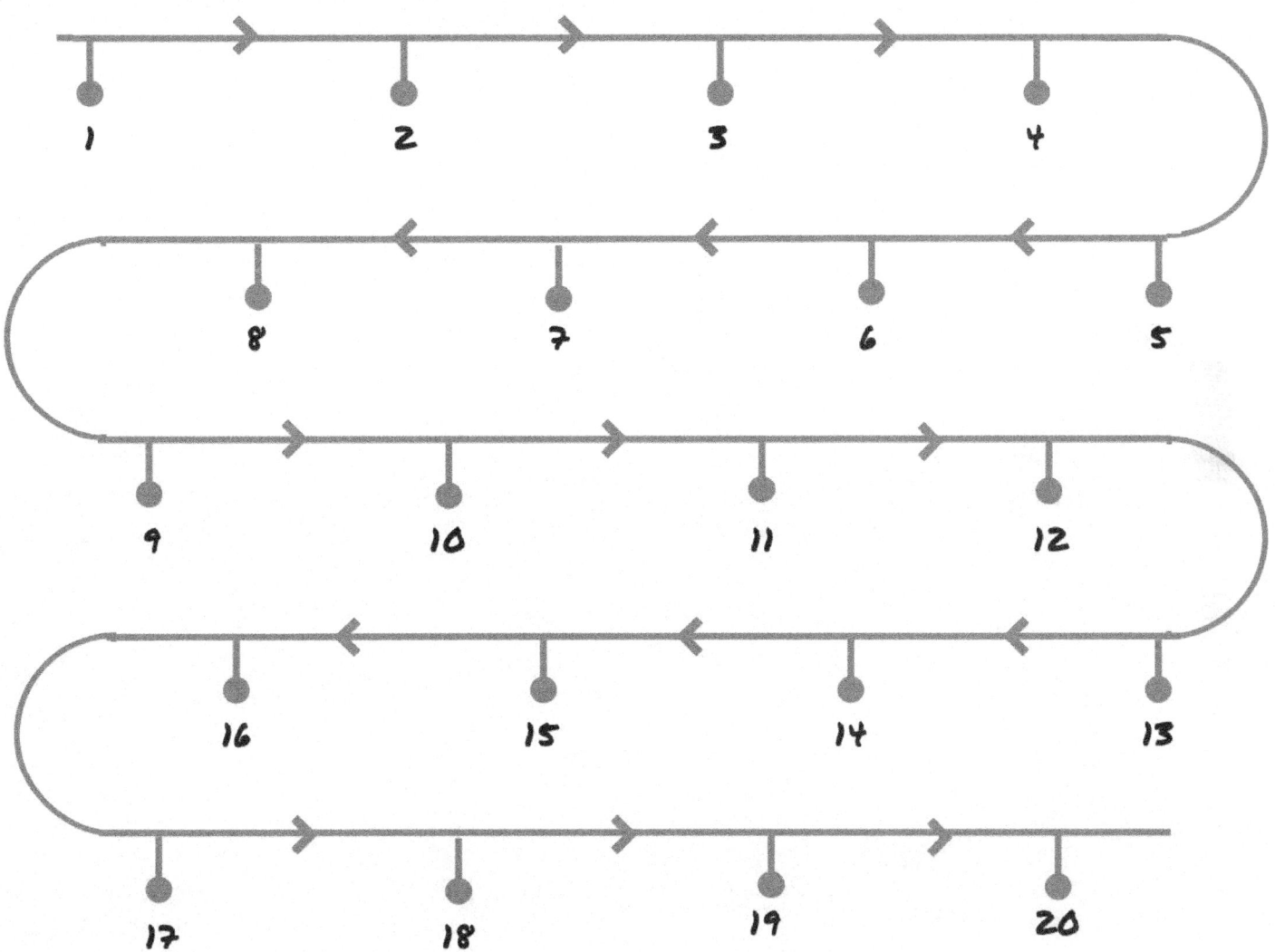

Rituals are the bridges that connect our intentions and aspirations with our habits, anchoring us to our values and guiding us towards our goals.

Unleashing Involuntary Yoga — Integrating Poses as Reflexes

Once you've mapped out the sequence of events for your average morning, I want you to circle the rituals where you think you could stack a yoga pose. You're unlikely to be doing one walking downstairs, (BTW, I know of someone who leaves a set of dumbbells at the top and bottom of their staircase and carries one up and down each time they take the stairs!), but you might when you put on your make-up.

It's no good selecting a ritual of plucking your eyebrows if you only do this every Saturday! If you want to create a long-term change, you need to pick the rituals that are consistently performed every day. As a reminder, mine looked like this.

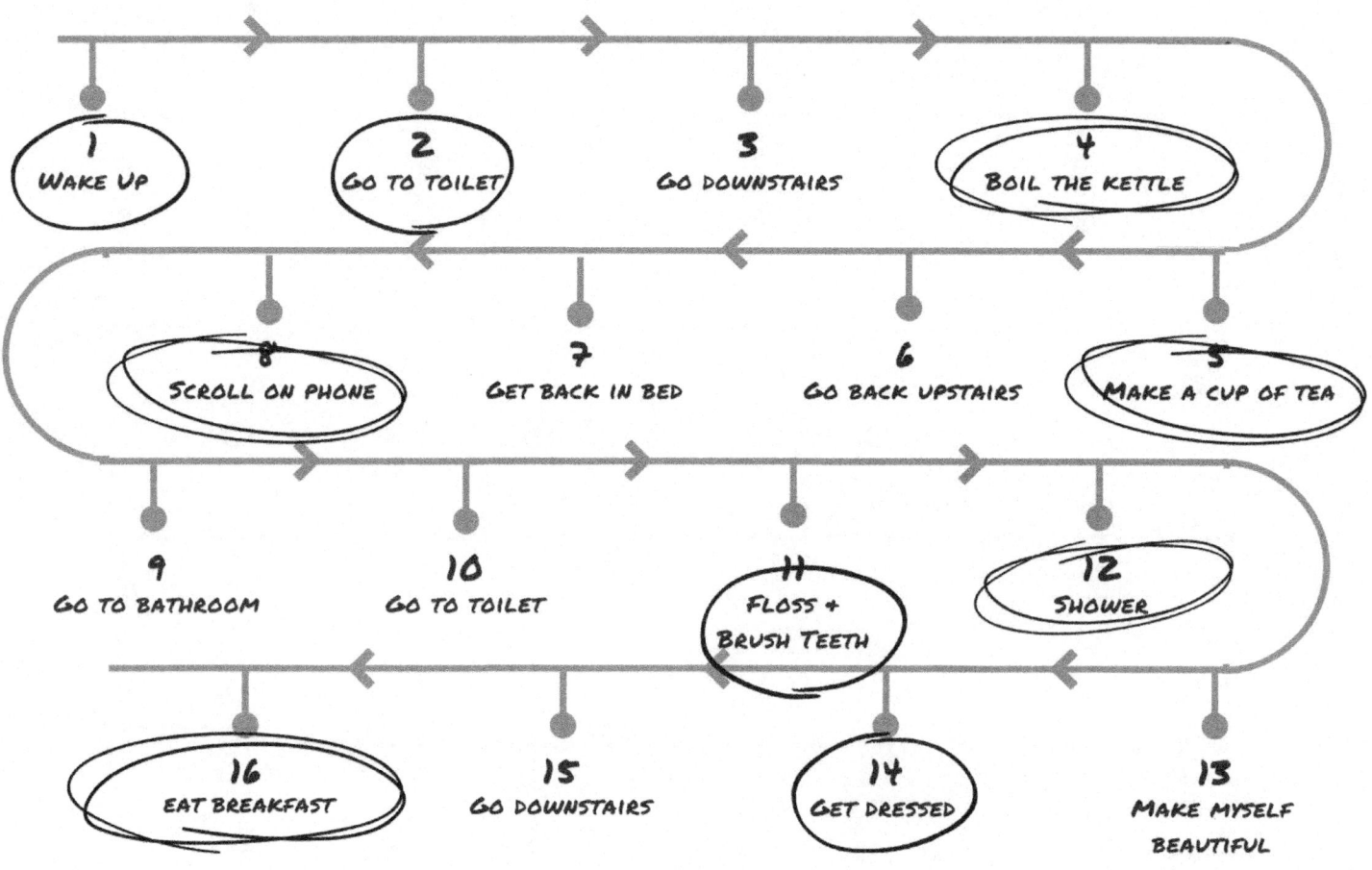

By building the repetition of yoga into your daily routines, you will soon develop an unconscious behaviour such as balancing on one foot every time you stand in a queue, when you pick up your bedside book just before sleep, you'll naturally take the butterfly position when settling down to read. This is known as automaticity — the quality or fact of being performed involuntarily or unconsciously, as a reflex, innate process, or ingrained habit.

STEP 4 — Creating your Personalised Morning Ritual

Take a piece of paper, a notepad, or the preformatted downloadable templates that can be accessed from Free Bonus Content in the Appendix.

Write the heading Morning Ritual at the top, and below that make a five-column table. In the first column write the heading Habit, followed by Ranking, Pose, Prompt and Reward as the other column headings.

Habit	Ranking	Pose	Prompt	Reward

The transformation from one state of being into another happens when we realise the abundance of our own potential.

Yoga Sutra 4.2

In the Habit column write down all the elements that you circled for your Morning Ritual on your Habit Flow Map. My table would look as follows:

My Habits
Wake up
Go to the toilet
Boil the kettle
Make a cup of tea
Scroll on phone in bed
Floss and brush teeth
Shower
Get dressed
Eat Breakfast

STEP 5 — The Power of Priority — Ranking Your Morning Habits

Think about which is the easiest habit you might be able to attach a Toothbrush Yoga pose to within your morning ritual. Is it when you wake up, brush your teeth, make a hot drink?

I want you to rank them in order of suitability for habit stacking or integration of a new Toothbrush Yoga habit. My recommendation is to start with brushing your teeth. You already do it twice a day, every day, which will help you with developing automaticity. It also only takes two minutes and I imagine you're normally on your own in a bathroom whilst doing it, so not many people will look at you oddly whilst you are practicing your pose.

The key is not to prioritise what's on your schedule but to schedule your priorities. - Stephen Covey

---

This is however *your* framework. There will be an aspect of *your* ritual that resonates most as the starting point. Whatever that is, in the second column (Ranking), write a number one in the adjacent column next to the habit that you want to start with.

Which one would be next? Write a two next to that, and so on until you have ranked the whole of your morning ritual. Here is my example ranking. Remember, yours should be whatever is most important to you to prioritise.

My Habits	Ranking
Wake up	3
Go to the toilet	4
Boil the kettle	5
Make a cup of tea	6
Scroll on phone in bed	2
Floss and brush teeth	1
Shower	9
Get dressed	7
Eat Breakfast	8

Where to Begin? — The Power of One Habit

You now have a running order of how to approach the gradual introduction of Toothbrush Yoga over the next few weeks or months, habit by habit. I'm not for a second suggesting that your morning ritual looks like mine on day one. Research has shown that if you want to adopt a new habit, it needs to be easy.

A journey of a thousand miles begins with a single step.

Lao Tzu

In a 12-week habit formation study involving 96 volunteers, outlined in — How are Habits Formed: Modelling Habit Formation in the Real World published in the European Journal of Social Psychology — participants were given the freedom to choose their own health-promoting behaviours. These ranged from straightforward actions like drinking a glass of water after breakfast to more intricate tasks such as completing 50 sit-ups. Notably, the study revealed that simpler behaviours were adopted much more quickly than their more complex counterparts.

Therefore, you must take the simplest aspects of your morning ritual first, as it will yield the quickest result. Instead of going through every ritual you have and attaching a Toothbrush Yoga pose to it on Day One, start with just one, the simplest!

Your morning ritual has been built up over years of ingrained repetition, expecting yourself to just remember to do this is a nigh-on impossibility.

STEP 6 — Strike a Pose

The next step is to choose which Toothbrush Pose(s) you will practice. The section later in this book called Toothbrush Yoga Pose Index is filled with a host of poses that can be practiced, as well as tips on how to do them. Do take a look at it for inspiration, or head to the YouTube Shorts videos at youtube.com/@toothbrushyoga. These are the poses that I perform within my framework:

Habit	Ranking	Pose	Position
Wake up	3	Child's Pose	
Go to the toilet (standing)	4	Mountain Pose on tip toes.	
Boil the kettle	5	Plank Pose, Downward Dog Pose followed by a Crescent Lunge Pose	
Make a cup of tea	6	Warrior 3 Pose	
Scroll on phone in bed	2	Reclining Bound Angle Pose	
Floss and brush teeth	1	Forward Fold Pose followed by a Half Lift Pose	
Shower	9	Eagle Pose	
Get dressed	7	Seated Pigeon Pose whilst putting on socks	
Eat breakfast	8	Seated Cat/Cow Pose	

Give some thought to what you will be doing during the habit and whether a standing, sitting, kneeling, or lying down pose would work best in that situation.

For example, it's unlikely that you'll be lying down flossing, so maybe a standing balance pose would work well. If you're just waking up, a lying down pose. In the third column under Pose, jot the pose(s) that you'd like to practice for each specific habit.

What does your table look like now?

Success is the product of daily habits, not once-in-a-lifetime transformations.

James Clear – Atomic Habits

STEP 7 — Harnessing the Power of Association

This is *the* most crucial point of the entire process, identifying a cue that will prompt your autopilot to interrupt its process and remember to practice the Toothbrush Yoga pose. This needs to be obvious. Let me say that again,

THIS NEEDS TO BE OBVIOUS!!!

The magic is in the prompt. There is a huge range of prompts that are available to you, be they time-based, location-based, object-based, situational, event-driven, visual, environmental, or physical.

- **Time-based** — in the world of Toothbrush Yoga, time-based prompts can be potent allies. They thrive on the regularity of your life, becoming ingrained in your daily rituals. When you associate a specific time with a particular behaviour, your brain learns to expect it, creating a natural rhythm in your routines. This predictability transforms seemingly ordinary moments into opportunities for intentional action. Anchoring a yoga pose to a specific time of the day—an 0800 morning stretch, a 1500 afternoon posture break, or a calming yoga session at 2300 before bedtime — these moments can integrate Toothbrush Yoga seamlessly into your schedule. Consider setting an alarm on your phone to be the time prompt you need?
- **Location-based** — your surroundings often serve as silent narrators, guiding your actions based on where you are. Location-based prompts are the geographical markers in your life, triggering specific behaviours tied to places. For example, the act of getting into bed could be your cue for practicing the Sphinx Pose.
- **Situational** — these are the contextual nuances that breathe life into habits. They arise from the circumstances you find yourselves in, these prompts are moulded by the situations you encounter, shaping your responses and steering you toward habitual actions, for example, sitting in a traffic jam or queuing for a bus.
- **Object-based** — throughout your day you will encounter objects that can be used as anchors to trigger behaviours. For example, before you go to bed, move the kettle to the kitchen table, which will prompt you to practice a Downward Dog Pose when you make your morning drink. I've been taking some joint supplements for years, and the only way I seem to be able to remember to take them is to put them in the drawer where I keep my deodorant. Despite what the research would suggest, I'm way past the 254 days of repetition, probably closer to 4000 days, but I seem to be immune from developing a habit around this, so I've anchored them to my deodorant. Every morning when I apply the spray there is a bag of tablets and that's the only way I seem to be able to remember to take one.
- **Event-driven** — events can often act as catalysts for your habits. The ring of a phone, a notification, an alarm — all these events can trigger habitual behaviours. Event-driven prompts are tied to specific occurrences, prompting you to respond in certain ways based on the unique nature of the event at hand. For example, the morning alarm might be the nudge you need to adopt Child's Pose. Maybe set a note in your work diary to remind you to include a pose at work or during the lunch break?
- **Visual** — these are the images, symbols, and colours that can interrupt your behaviours. They can range from a Post-it note to a yoga mat rolled out in the corner of the room. Visual cues tap

into your subconscious, communicating messages that guide your habits through the power of sight. For example, you could place an elastic band, a sticker, or some Sellotape around the handle of the toothbrush. When you next go to brush your teeth, seeing the elastic band/sticker/Sellotape will trigger the recall to practice the Toothbrush Yoga pose. Buy a set of colourful fun shaped Post-it notes and write fun messages to yourself around the house?

- **Environmental** — environmental prompts are inspired by the things that are around us. If every morning you smell your coffee brewing, this could be your cue to practice the Happy Baby Pose whilst in bed.
- **Physical** — your body is the vessel of your sensory experiences, and physical cues harness these sensations to trigger habits. If every time you're feeling thirsty, or the urge to smoke, these physical sensations become cues, prompting specific actions. Physical cues are deeply intertwined with the tactile and kinaesthetic aspects of your daily life, initiating habits through the language of sensation.

Cues are the keys that unlock your potential for growth and transformation.

Here are a few ideas:

- Wake up — set an alarm that makes a different sound or better still a verbal instruction to practice a certain Toothbrush Yoga pose.
- Go to the toilet — put a sticker/Post-it on the toilet lid/cistern.
- Go downstairs and boil the kettle — leave the kettle in a different place.
- Make a cup of tea/coffee — put another object in your cutlery drawer where you keep the spoons, or something out of place, like a golf ball in the jar you get the tea/coffee from.
- Go back upstairs, get back in bed and pick up your phone — have the background of your phone saying a phrase like TOOTHBRUSH YOGA
- Floss — put the floss in a different location, in the bedroom for example, rather than the bathroom, once you've pulled off the tape, leave it back in that place.
- Brush teeth — place an elastic band on the toothbrush handle.
- Have a shower — place an elastic band around the shower gel container.
- Making yourself even more beautiful — put a note inside wherever it is that you take the products from.
- Get dressed — a note inside the sock draw.
- Go downstairs and eat breakfast — a note stuck to the breakfast cereal.

I can't impress upon you enough: it is all in the cue/prompts. Doing the Toothbrush Yoga pose is the simple bit, interrupting your habits to instigate the pose is the difficult bit, but it's critical for achieving the transformation. The key is consistency; as these poses become integrated into your morning ritual, they'll become a natural and indispensable part of your day.

Cues are the signals that prompt our habits. By understanding and controlling our cues, we can shape our behaviours.

Charles Duhigg — The Power of Habit

Now it is your turn. In the fourth column of your table under the Prompt column, write out what will trigger you to remember to practice the pose. I've given some examples in the table below.

Habit	Ranking	Pose	Prompt
Wake up	3	Child's Pose	Set an Alarm
Go to the toilet (standing)	4	Mountain Pose on tip toes.	Place a Post-it note on the toilet
Boil the kettle	5	Plank Pose, Downward Dog Pose followed by a Crescent Lunge Pose	Leave the kettle in a different place.
Make a cup of tea	6	Warrior 3 Pose	Put a golf ball in the cutlery draw
Scroll on phone in bed	2	Reclining Bound Angle Pose	Use the Toothbrush Yoga screensaver
Floss and brush teeth	1	Forward Fold Pose followed by a Half Lift Pose	Leave the floss in the bedroom
Shower	9	Eagle Pose	Put an elastic band on the shower gel
Get dressed	7	Seated Pigeon Pose whilst putting on socks	Place a note in the drawer
Eat breakfast	8	Seated Cat/Cow Pose	Keep the bowls in a different cupboard

STEP 8 — Reaping the Rewards

The final step in the Habit Flow is to determine what reward you will associate with the practice. It's not the size of the reward that matters most; it's the sensation it evokes within you. It doesn't matter what it is, it's the act itself that counts.

Reward your efforts, not just your accomplishments.

In the fifth column of your table, under the Reward heading, note down how you will recognise your achievement. Here are a few reward ideas:

- Smile in the mirror and appreciate your progress.
- Reward yourself with a small piece of dark chocolate or a healthy snack.
- Take a luxurious warm shower or bath as a form of self-care.
- Look in the mirror and give yourself a genuine compliment.
- Set a new goal or intention for your next yoga practice.
- Write a positive affirmation related to your accomplishment and repeat it to yourself.
- Give yourself a high-five or a fist pump.
- Write down your achievements in your yoga journal.
- Place a piece of pasta in a jar so you can visually see your achievements grow.
- Listen to your favourite uplifting song or playlist.
- Share your accomplishment on social media and bask in the positive feedback.
- Repeat one of your positive mantras.
- Take a deep breath and savour the sense of accomplishment.

The biggest reward in life is not what you get, but who you become.

Unknown

Remember, these rewards are customisable, and you can mix and match them based on your preferences.

The key is to choose rewards that bring you joy and reinforce your sense of accomplishment after achieving a yoga pose. Mine are as follows:

Habit	Ranking	Pose	Prompt	Reward
Wake up	3	Child's Pose	Set an Alarm	Affirmation out loud, "Today is gonna be a great day"
Go to the toilet (standing)	4	Mountain Pose on tip toes.	Place a Post-it note on the toilet	Conscious breath as I feel the sense the relief
Boil the kettle	5	Plank Pose, Downward Dog Pose followed by a Crescent Lunge Pose	Leave the kettle in a different place.	Noticing how my body feels after the stretch
Make a cup of tea	6	Warrior 3 Pose	Put a golf ball in the cutlery draw	Noticing the warmth of the cup in my hands
Scroll on phone in bed	2	Reclining Bound Angle Pose	Use the Toothbrush Yoga screensaver	Allowing the relaxation of my muscles in bed
Floss and brush teeth	1	Forward Fold Pose followed by a Half Lift Pose	Leave the floss in the bedroom	Enjoying the refreshing taste of the minty toothpaste
Shower	9	Eagle Pose	Put an elastic band on the shower gel	Relishing the feel of the water on my skin
Get dressed	7	Seated Pigeon Pose whilst putting on socks	Place a note in the drawer	Wriggling my toes in the comfort of a fresh pair of socks gives
Eat breakfast	8	Seated Cat/Cow Pose	Keep the bowls in a different cupboard	Ticking off all the completed poses on my Habit Trackers

STEP 9 — Continuing the Flow — Evening Ritual and Beyond

Once you've had a go at your Morning Ritual, I recommend that you repeat the same process for your Work/Study, Everyday and Evening Rituals. Start a fresh Habit Flow Map for each of them and plan out the habit, ranking, pose, prompt, and reward in tables as we have just done for the morning routine.

Repetition, Repetition, Repetition

You now have your Toothbrush Yoga intentions mapped out. Start small, and find one habit, one moment in your day, where you can seamlessly incorporate a yoga pose. Choosing that specific ritual where you'll practice a yoga pose, practice the same pose every time. It does not have to be long. Maybe 15 - 30 seconds to start with, depending on the one and depending on your body? Consistency is key to forming a habit. If you vary the pose, you'll vary the results of building the habit. Let it become as automatic as brushing your teeth. Once it's deeply rooted, feel free to vary it, then introduce another, and then another and so on.

It's not about how long you have been building the habit, it's entirely about the frequency of repeating it.

As you've seen from the science, there is no right answer to how many repetitions you need to do to develop a habit. You simply need to do it enough times for it to become ingrained. This goes back to having the identity of a Toothbrush Yogi, engage in this every day for three months and see for yourself if unbeknown to you, you will become that Yogi!

In the first couple of weeks, I recommend you stick to the same pose(s) for each element of your defined ritual to build the consistent repetition that will ingrain Toothbrush Yoga into your subconscious. Just be cautious not to overdo it and injure yourself. When you start this process, you will need to consciously remember and concentrate on how to practice the pose, working on the alignment of your lower, mid, and upper body sections. Once the habit is ingrained, it's time to move on to the next habit/pose.

Remember, you're trying to build a framework of lifestyle improvements; the snowball needs the momentum to roll down the hill. It is for you to decide how fast.

If you want to accelerate the adoption of more poses, you can either move on to the next ranking on your list or introduce another ritual. The only caution is the adaptability of your body.

The key is to start. Start today. Start small. Just start.

Unknown

Refine and Evolve

Once you have ingrained the habit that when you floss for example, you will practice a standing balance pose, then you can choose to switch it up — perhaps doing the Tree Pose, a Warrior 3 Pose, or any other balance pose. Developing variations will help increase your suppleness and strength. Be sure to balance both the left and right sides. After time, and practice, the habit will be formed and taking the pose will become automated, but please don't forget to pay attention to your body's alignment.

Soon, you'll find that yoga isn't something you do; it's something you are. It's in the way you breathe, the way you move, and the way you approach life. It's a journey of self-discovery, of mindful living, and of holistic well-being. Embrace the process, and let the results take care of themselves. Your body, mind, and spirit will thank you for it. By incorporating these principles, yoga can seamlessly become a part of your daily rituals.

Once the habit is built, you could just coast on autopilot, or you can continue to build and develop your practice further, perhaps developing a mindful approach to the task/pose you are performing.

You can take it a step further and focus on mindfulness with each pose. If you're brushing your teeth, you could mindfully become aware of your teeth, your gums, your breath, the plaque on your teeth, and your body. You can take this in any direction and deepen your practice, exploring new poses and techniques to keep it engaging and enjoyable. By continuously evaluating and developing your yoga practice you will become an expert in what you do.

You will never change your life until you change something you do daily. The secret of your success is found in your daily routine.

John C. Maxwell

STEP 10 — Plotting and Tracking the Milestones

Knowing how the process of habit transformation unfolds, you now have the power to take control of it. You have developed your thinking around the outcomes you want to achieve, conceived of your new identity, and mapped out the rituals and poses you wish you prioritise and therefore you have a plan of how to introduce the changes that you want to achieve. It's now time to set yourself some goals. Goals will help clarify your intentions, make progress measurable, and keep you accountable. By setting goals, you create the means to navigate your journey for self-improvement and transformation.

A goal without a plan is just a wish!

Your goals need to seamlessly align with both the outcomes and identity that you've set. If your outcome is to achieve physical and mental balance through yoga, and your identity is being a mindful yogi, your goals should create a harmonious synergy, reinforcing your commitment to your desired outcomes.

Setting clear and achievable goals is one of the cornerstones of your Toothbrush Yoga framework.

Documenting your goals provides you with direction, motivation, and a measurable way to track your progress, whilst also reinforcing the likelihood of achieving them.

Psychology professor Dr Gail Matthews of the Dominican University ran a goal-setting study in California involving 267 participants. Dr Matthew found that people were 42% more likely to achieve their goals just by writing them down. Writing down your goals is therefore a great way not just to track progress but increase your chances of success.

The process of putting pen to paper helps articulate your goals, making them tangible, actionable, and more likely to succeed.

One of the main reasons is due to the process of encoding. When information is recorded via handwriting instead of just thinking about it or reading it, it is easier for the data to be retained. This clarifies why note-taking can enhance studying, understanding new ideas, and memorising. Hence why note taking has been proven to aid with memorising, learning and studying.

Duration of Goals

Goals can vary in duration, depending on their nature and complexity. There are no weekly, monthly or annual goals in Toothbrush Yoga. Creating a goal structure that is defined in specific durations goes against the whole objective of the book. You are focused on incremental change over a long period. Therefore, there are only two timeframes that I want you to consider – short-term and long-term – to strike a balance between consistent progress and long-term vision.

Where to Start?

By prioritising the destination in your mind, you empower yourself to strategically place markers along the route, enabling you to navigate and track your progress effectively.

Start with the end in mind.

- **Long-term goals** — encompass a broader perspective and a more comprehensive approach. They guide your overall yoga journey and provide a framework for setting shorter-term objectives. Long-term goals align with your greater vision and serve as a guiding force throughout your practice.
- **Short-term goals** — focus on quick wins, allowing you to break progress into manageable steps, providing you with quick wins, boosting your confidence and motivation.

My own yoga goals are shown below, some short-term (ST), and some long-term (LT); the short-term ones are much more achievable!

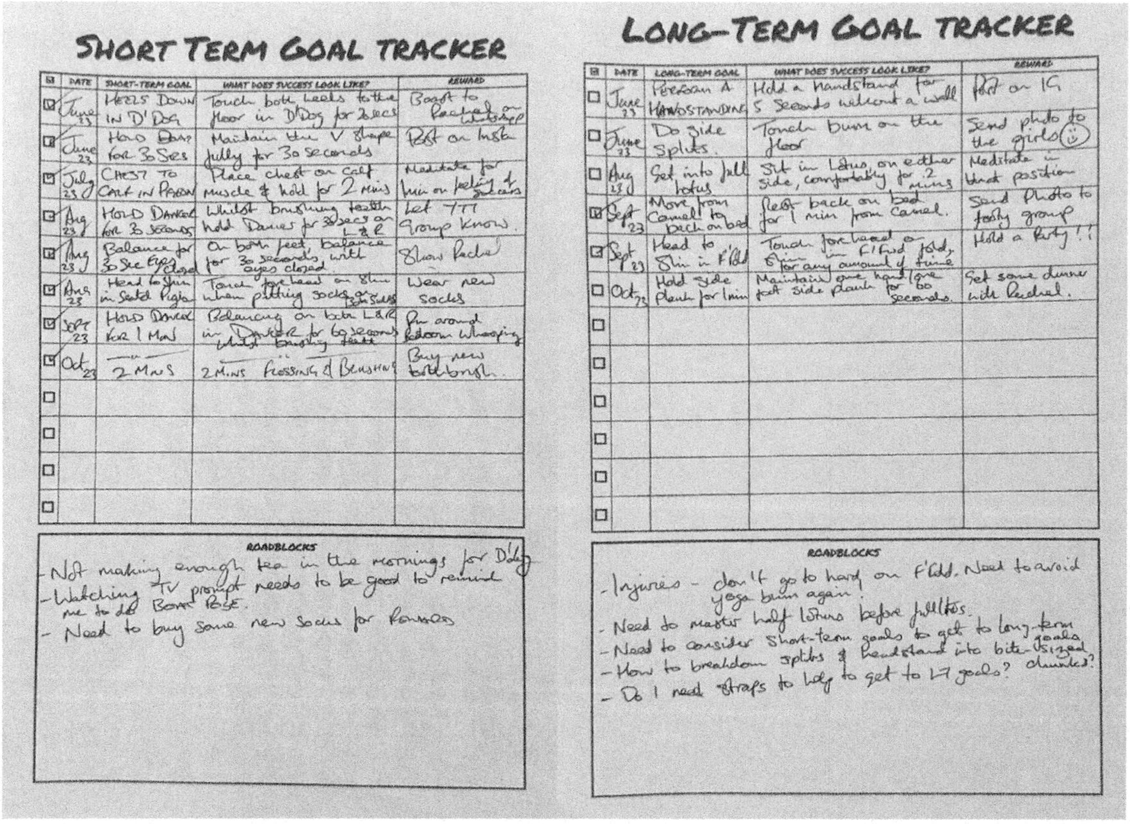

I have been able to observe my progress over a six-month period and have achieved all my short-term goals. As someone with no previous yoga experience and barely able to do a Downward Dog Pose, I'm now able to touch my heels down on the floor. Likewise, six months ago I was barely able to balance in the Dancer Pose, yet now I'm able to floss my teeth on one leg for two minutes.

As I'm now doing yoga within my rituals I mentally record where my body is at each and every day. I am constantly aware of what range of movement I have. If I've not practiced a Downward Dog Pose for a few days, I struggle to get my heels down, unless I adjust the angle of my pose (top tip for a little cheating 😊).

Goal Setting within the Toothbrush Yoga Framework

Goals within the Toothbrush Yoga framework sit beneath each of the moments in your day when you determine there is an opportunity for habit stacking. Each routine for which you have chosen a pose to practice presents the opportunity to create a specific goal, either short or long-term. It's entirely up to you whether you choose one or multiple goals, I've expanded my own goals in the diagram below for two of the moments in my day.

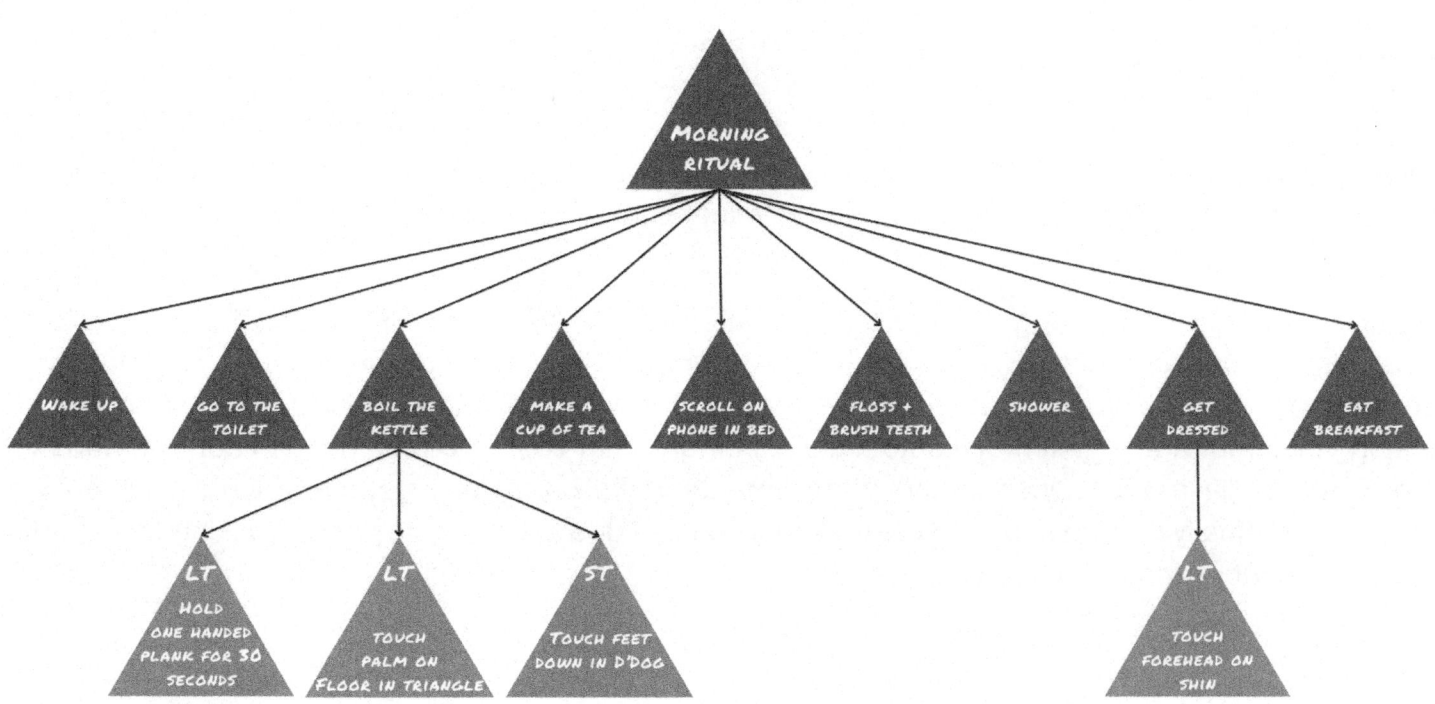

Reflect and Visualise

Take a moment to reflect on your current aspirations and where you would like to see yourself in the future. Visualise your yoga practice and its impact on various areas of your life, such as physical, mental, emotional, and spiritual well-being. Use this insight to form a clear picture of your goals.

SMAR not SMART Goals

When you start tracking your progress with goals you may wish to consider the SMART technique for goal tracking - Specific, Measurable, Achievable, Relevant, and Time-bound. The technique helps ensure your goals are realistic. They should also be Specific and Relevant to your overall objective and well-being, however, the most important aspect here is Achievable. Be sure to set *your* goals small, just a single bite, and plan on having lots of them. There is nothing like the feeling of attaining your goal for that hit of dopamine.

One of my first goals was to be able to touch my heels down on the floor while doing downward dog. I'll never forget the day when my heels connected with the floor that first time in a Downward Dog Pose during my yoga teacher training. Moments like this propelled me forward.

I also encourage you to drop the "T" Time-bound aspect of SMART. Toothbrush Yoga is focused on long-term transformation, not Time-Bound achievements. As with any formidable challenge, it's essential to approach it methodically, acknowledging that it's not the speed but the repetition of bites that will lead to devouring the elephant.

What specific changes do you want to see in your life through Toothbrush Yoga?

Begin by reflecting on your desired outcomes that you have already written down. Whether it's improved elasticity, reduced stress, enhanced mindfulness, or overall well-being, think clearly about the outcomes you're aiming for.

Break down your long-term goals into smaller, manageable steps. If you want to Plank Pose for 30 seconds but you can't hold your own weight in the plank position, this must be broken down into several smaller bites. Start by doing a standing plank against a wall by creating an angle of 60 degrees and leaning into your arms, next move onto a Dolphin Plank with your forearms on the floor, (perhaps you also need to have your knees touching the floor as well). From here you can then straighten your arms/knees, finally moving into a full plank. These smaller goals act as milestones, making your journey more achievable and less overwhelming.

When it is obvious that the goals cannot be reached, don't adjust the goals, adjust the action steps.

Confucius

This incremental approach allows you to integrate Toothbrush Yoga seamlessly into your existing habits. Just like changing your habits, instead of overwhelming changes, focus on small, consistent actions that contribute to your desired outcomes.

Consider the Roadblocks

Goals, no matter how well-defined, are not immune to challenges. Life is filled with unexpected twists and turns, and it's essential to anticipate potential roadblocks before they even appear on the horizon. In their book — New Developments in Goal Setting and Task Performance — researchers, Edwin Locke, and Gray Latham, believe that identifying obstacles before setting any goal is essential. It's a bit like having Google Maps for your goals, helping to develop resilience ahead of future obstacles.

When setting your Toothbrush Yoga goals, it's valuable to engage in proactive foresight.

Consider the hurdles you might encounter along the way. These roadblocks could be anything from unexpected work commitments and family obligations to fatigue and moments of self-doubt. By acknowledging these potential challenges in advance, you empower yourself to devise strategies to overcome them.

Begin by listing out in your notebook the obstacles that could hinder your progress. Is it a lack of time? Demands from work or family? Physical discomfort? By pinpointing these challenges, you're acknowledging their existence and refusing to be blindsided when they arise.

For each identified roadblock, create a contingency plan. If time constraints are an issue, perhaps you could wake up a few minutes earlier? If fatigue is a concern, consider incorporating energising poses into your routine to invigorate your body and mind. If your children interrupt your morning routines, perhaps the evening is the best time to start when they are in bed.

By considering potential roadblocks in advance and preparing for them, you empower yourself to navigate the twists and turns of life with grace and determination.

Remember, challenges are not dead ends; they are merely detours that can lead you to new discoveries and deeper resilience. Embrace them as opportunities for growth and let your Toothbrush Yoga practice flourish even in the face of adversity.

Tracking Progress

In the early days, I strongly recommend keeping a record of your progress. This isn't the same as setting goals, but by tracking your progress, it will provide valuable insights into your patterns, progress, and areas for improvement.

By visually seeing your habits over time, you become more accountable and can easily identify trends that may impact reaching your goals. A simple tick list works well as a method of recording your habit streaks. The insights gained will help you refine your future goals. This can be weekly, monthly, quarterly, or whatever timeframe `makes sense to you.

Most people overestimate what they can do in a week or a month, but they massively underestimate what they can accomplish in a decade.

For my own purposes, I record my progress monthly, against each of the rituals that I have. As you can see from the chart below, I'm great and habit stacking in my dental and bed routines. I don't always remember to practice when I wake up, but that could be due to the day I have ahead of me. I'm also much better at doing my practice at weekends. You can also see that I'm not the one who makes the tea in the morning! As I told you, real insights, Rachel wasn't very impressed when she saw this! 😊

Another great motivation area is setting a streak challenge. Take the Toothbrush Challenge and see if you can practice for 30 consecutive days of yoga whilst brushing your teeth.

30-day challenges are a great way to combine a target and motivation. Can you maintain a certain level of consistency for a whole month?

Review and Reset

Periodically, every month, quarter, or six monthly, review your goals and the progress made. Reflect on your long-term ambitions and see if your short-term ambitions are taking you in that direction. Life is dynamic, and so are your priorities. Adapting your goals ensures they remain relevant to your evolving journey. The Toothbrush Yoga approach is about flexibility, both physically and metaphorically, allowing you to weave yoga into the fabric of your life.

Perfection is a myth; progress is the reality that transforms dreams into achievements.

Embracing the Journey — Progress Over Perfection

Goal setting is a vibrant process that fuels your yoga practice with intention and purpose. By being mindful of the duration of goals and following this approach, you can harness the power of goal setting to manifest transformative changes in your yoga journey.

As you progress your Toothbrush Yoga adventure, every pose becomes an opportunity for self-discovery and growth, reinforcing your commitment. Progress over perfection, mindfulness over monotony, and gentle persistence over intense effort.

Toothbrush Yoga is not about achieving perfection in specific poses but about embodying a balanced lifestyle.

The true magic lies not in the goals you set, but in the framework itself. Your journey becomes your destination. Remain adaptable in your goal-setting process. Be open to modifying your goals based on your evolving needs and experiences. Flexibility ensures that your goals remain relevant and achievable.

Determining your Toothbrush Yoga goals is a deeply personal and empowering process. By setting clear, SMAR goals, breaking them down into manageable steps, and aligning them with your habits, you pave the way for transformative results. Embrace your unique goals, stay focused, and celebrate every step of your Toothbrush Yoga journey toward holistic well-being and self-discovery.

When it comes to transforming our own minds, changing our habits, or settling into a new routine, we must let go of the past, focus on what we can do in the present, and surrender to whatever the future holds.

Ashley Zuberi

Chapter 9: The Power of Journaling

Journaling provides a platform for self-reflection. By documenting your thoughts, emotions, and experiences, you gain deeper insights into your physical, mental, and emotional states. Through the act of writing, your intentions, thoughts, aspirations, and actions converge, providing you with invaluable insights into your progress. These headings will help you monitor your feelings over time:

- **A line-a-day** — a simple yet powerful practice that involves capturing the essence of our daily experiences in just a sentence or two. It involves distilling our thoughts, emotions, and events into concise snippets that capture the essence of each day. With this practice, we can reflect on both mundane and remarkable moments, cultivating gratitude, self-awareness, and mindfulness. A line-a-day journal allows us to create a tangible record of our lives, providing a space for introspection, personal growth, and the opportunity to look back and appreciate the journey we have embarked upon. By committing to this daily habit, we invite a sense of presence and intention into our lives.
- **Daily progress** — dedicate sections in your journal to record your yoga practice during different daily routines. Describe the poses performed, the challenges faced, and the rewards experienced. Note the cues, cravings, and responses you encounter. As you record your progress, setbacks, and achievements, you create a visual timeline of your journey.
- **Weekly progress** — at the end of each week, reflect on your progress. Note any improvements, challenges overcome, or new poses you've incorporated. Journaling will help you recognise patterns or defects in your system. If you keep forgetting to practice when you brush your teeth, is it because your prompt isn't specific enough? It might need to be more than just when you brush your teeth, you might need to be specific — such as when you taste the minty toothpaste, which might then signal you to practice a Tree Pose. It's not when you finish your workday, it's when you physically close your laptop, which signals the prompt to practice a Seated Cat/Cow Pose.
- **Reflections and celebrations** — conclude your journal entries with regular reflections. How did the day's yoga practice make you feel? What insights did you gain? Celebrate your achievements, no matter how small, and acknowledge the obstacles you overcame. For those who get great joy from ticking off a checklist, why not create one in your journal to see how many of your poses you achieved that day? This will give a clear visual of progress over time too.

Unless you journal already today, this will need to develop into another habit, so start small. Journal for no more than 120 seconds and let it develop into an intrinsic part of your Toothbrush Yoga routine. Perhaps this is the last thing you do at night as you ease back into a relaxing pose?

Your journal is a personal space. Be honest with yourself, acknowledge your struggles, and celebrate your victories.

A Line A Day

JAN FEB MAR APR MAY JUN
JUL AUG SEP OCT NOV DEC

| 1/ |
| 2/ |
| 3/ |
| 4/ |
| 5/ |
| 6/ |
| 7/ |
| 8/ |
| 9/ |
| 10/ |
| 11/ |
| 12/ |
| 13/ |
| 14/ |
| 15/ |
| 16/ |
| 17/ |
| 18/ |
| 19/ |
| 20/ |
| 21/ |
| 22/ |
| 23/ |
| 24/ |
| 25/ |
| 26/ |
| 27/ |
| 28/ |
| 29/ |
| 30/ |
| 31/ |

Daily Progress

Today's Date:

Today I am feeling:

Poses:

Challenges & Triumphs:

Rewards:

Weekly Progress

Week:

Thoughts on the week:

Improvements:

Challenges & Triumphs:

Goals check-in:

Reflections & Celebrations

Chapter 10: Counting the Streak — The Power of Habit-Tracking Apps

Smartphones have become indispensable tools for enhancing various aspects of our lives, including our wellness journey. As an alternative or complement to a physical journal, habit-tracking apps have emerged as powerful allies in the quest for personal growth, offering seamless ways to record progress, stay accountable, and cultivate consistency.

Habit-tracking apps simplify the process of monitoring your Toothbrush Yoga practice. With just a few taps, you can log the yoga poses you've performed, the duration of each session, and any additional notes about your experience. These apps provide a visual representation of your progress, allowing you to see how far you've come and motivating you to continue your journey.

Choosing the Right App

I suggest you explore various habit-tracking apps available on your smartphone's app store. Look for user-friendly interfaces, customisable features, and positive reviews from the wellness community. Find an app that resonates with your preferences and aligns with your goals.

My personal favourites from the free-of-charge ones on IOS are Habit, Done, Habit Tracker and HabitKit. There are many others, however, so feel free to experiment.

Motivational Notifications

It's possible to set personalised reminders and notifications within habit-tracking apps. These gentle nudges serve as cues, prompting you to engage in your Toothbrush Yoga practice. Whether it's a morning reminder to stretch or an evening prompt for relaxation poses, these notifications keep yoga at the forefront of your mind, making it easier to integrate into your daily routines.

Streak Tracking for Consistency

Habit-tracking apps often feature streak counters, celebrating the consecutive days you've practiced. Streaks are powerful motivators, instilling a sense of achievement and encouraging you to maintain your consistency. As your streak grows, so does your confidence and commitment to your practice.

Streaks are the footprints on the path to mastery. Let each day be a step closer to the yogi you're becoming.

Visual Progress Indicators

Many apps offer visual representations of your progress, such as charts, graphs, or calendar views. Seeing your yoga journey unfold in a tangible format provides a sense of accomplishment and reinforces your dedication encouraging you to continue stacking Toothbrush Yoga into your routines.

Community Support and Accountability

Some habit-tracking apps enable you to join communities or share your progress with friends. More of this in Chapter 11: How to Shape Your Habits — Social Accountability — Try This With Your Friends!

Notes

Chapter 11: How to Shape Your Habits — Social Accountability — Try This With Your Friends!

Embracing social accountability in Toothbrush Yoga transforms the solitary path of habit-building into a shared adventure. The shared commitment, the mutual celebration of achievements, and the collective resilience in the face of challenges elevate the journey. In this interconnected network of support, Toothbrush Yoga becomes more than a personal practice — it becomes a shared voyage towards holistic well-being, one pose at a time.

> *When you share your Toothbrush Yoga endeavours with others, you create a web of accountability, motivation, and inspiration.*

The simple act of voicing your goals and progress to friends, family, or a supportive community fosters a sense of responsibility and commitment, magnifying the meaning, and significantly increasing the likelihood that your Toothbrush Yoga practice will endure.

That said, Toothbrush Yoga is entirely based on *your* rituals alone. Attaching a pose to *your* day-to-day routines involves no one other than you.

So how can you build accountability to support you?

Create a Shared Journey

Share your Toothbrush Yoga journey with your family and friends. Invite them to join you in your practices or simply inform them about your goals. When your close ones are aware of your endeavours, they can offer encouragement and understanding, fostering a supportive environment.

Your commitment becomes a shared endeavour, strengthening the resolve of both parties. The shared accountability creates a ripple effect, where your dedication motivates others, and their progress fuels your determination.

Accountability Partnerships

Consider partnering with a friend or family member who wants to make their own lifestyle improvements. Set mutual goals and hold each other accountable. Regular check-ins and shared progress can boost motivation and make the habit more enjoyable.

Accountability is the glue that ties commitment to results.

Bob Proctor

Social Media Synergy — Strengthening Toothbrush Yoga Habits with Online Communities

In the digital age, social circles extend far beyond our immediate family and friends. Online platforms and social media communities offer a vast landscape to foster social accountability.

The people we connect with digitally significantly shape our habits. Knowing that others are witnessing your journey creates a sense of responsibility, encouraging you to stay consistent.

> *Engaging with like-minded individuals, sharing your daily practices, and celebrating each other's victories can amplify your commitment to Toothbrush Yoga.*

Harness the Hashtags

Embrace the hashtag #toothbrushyoga as your digital rallying point. By using this hashtag, you join a community of like-minded individuals worldwide. Share your yoga poses, your progress, and your thoughts on how Toothbrush Yoga enriches your life. The hashtag serves as a beacon, guiding you to others who share your passion and goals.

Daily Inspirational Posts

Follow @toothbrushyoga on both Instagram and TikTok to see how to practice the poses detailed within this book, including variations to the poses, how to move from beginner to advanced stages of the poses, motivational quotes, and how to fix various body challenges, such as a sore lower back etc.

You're An Inspiration to Others

Daily posting of your journey not only reinforces your commitment but also encourages and acts as an inspiration to others in the Toothbrush Yoga community. Your positivity becomes contagious, motivating others to embrace their practice as well.

Inspiring others is not just about where you are, but about where you have come from and the journey you've travelled.

Unknown

Progress Journals/Visual Diaries

Beyond the journaling previously suggested you could also capture your Toothbrush Yoga journey visually. Post pictures or short videos showcasing your progress. Seeing your journey unfold on screen can not only boost your confidence but also serve as a testament to the power of consistent practice, inspiring others in the community.

By engaging with the #toothbrushyoga community on social media, you transform your digital interactions into powerful catalysts for your Toothbrush Yoga habits. Your online presence becomes a source of inspiration, and the collective energy of the community bolsters your resolve.

Together, you and your online companions form a virtual "sangha", a community that uplifts, motivates, and celebrates every step of your Toothbrush Yoga journey.

Through the synergy of technology and mindfulness, you discover that the digital world can be a sanctuary, nurturing your Toothbrush Yoga habits and amplifying the impact of your practice.

Notes

Chapter 12: Don't Over Do It!

In the exhilarating journey of Toothbrush Yoga, enthusiasm can sometimes lead us down a slippery slope. Eager to witness quick results, you might be tempted to push yourself beyond your limits, forcing stretches and contortions that your body isn't ready for. While dedication is commendable, it's equally crucial to exercise caution and practice mindfulness. Here's why moderation matters and how to find the perfect balance in your practice.

If you fall over, you fall over. If you have to stop, you stop. But you start again. Just like life itself, you start again.

Gurmukh Kaur Khalsa

Warm-up and Cool-down

Since Toothbrush Yoga poses are linked to existing habits, rather than an exercise class, there is no designated warm-up or cool-down. It is therefore essential to approach your practice mindfully to prevent injuries. Here are some key pointers:

Don't Push Too Hard

Yoga poses involve sustained stretching, coaxing muscles to lengthen gradually. As you hold a stretch, the muscle fibres adjust and elongate, increasing their elasticity. Over time, this enhanced elasticity allows muscles to lengthen further without causing strain or injury.

Pushing your body too hard, especially during the early stages, in the pursuit of flexibility, can lead to injuries. Injuries not only cause physical pain but can also demotivate and derail your practice, halting your development altogether.

Injury is not a setback; it is an opportunity to deepen your understanding of your body and cultivate a more mindful approach to your yoga practice.

Ease into each pose gently, deepening the pose with your breath. Your body communicates with you during every pose. It tells you when a stretch feels intense but beneficial and when it's too much. Learn to discern these signals. Pain is not what you should be experiencing and is certainly not a prerequisite for progress. Instead, focus on finding a comfortable edge in each pose.

With consistent practice, your body will naturally open up, allowing you to delve deeper into poses over time. If you have any stabbing or shooting pain (upwards or downwards), numbness or tingling, or sudden loss of bowel or bladder control stop doing what you're doing!

Discomfort is to be expected but yoga often refers to finding your 'edge'. This is discomfort without pain. If a particular stretch feels too intense, back off slightly. The essence of Toothbrush Yoga lies in gentle, gradual progress.

Your body is your best guide. It constantly tells you, in the form of pain or sensations, what's working for you and what's not.

Hina Hashmi

Be Cautious in Back Bends

Be considerate of your back, particularly your lower back. Some of the backbends in the Yoga Index are deeper than others. As you start on your yoga path begin with Sphinx Pose and move on from there. If you have pain, STOP!

Every back bend is an invitation to let go of what holds you back, making space for renewed energy and vitality."

It's Okay to Not Be Perfect

Anyone who ever started yoga had to start somewhere. It's OK not to be perfect. It's OK if you get tired or frustrated. It's OK if you're not that flexible!

I hadn't been to a single yoga class before I ended up on a three-day retreat! Less than 10 lessons later I was starting a 200-hour Yoga Teacher Training course, and the funny thing was, I wasn't even the worst in the class, which surprised the heck out of me. 😊

Yoga is not about reaching perfection, but about embracing the imperfections and finding peace within them in your journey.

Start Small and Slow

Begin your Toothbrush Yoga journey with simple poses and gentle movements. Focus on the basics, ensuring you maintain proper form and alignment. Gradually introduce more complex poses as your body becomes accustomed to the practice. Small, consistent efforts yield significant results over time. Remember, this is a journey, not a race. Allow your body the time it needs to adapt and grow.

Utilise Props and Modifications

Props like blocks, straps, or cushions can aid in achieving proper alignment and provide support during poses. Don't hesitate to use them if you would like to, though this book is designed for you to incorporate yoga poses as simply as possible.

If you're new to yoga, or lack flexibility in certain areas, when you follow the step-by-step guides, you might not be able to perform the pose as per the images. It doesn't matter. Just like in a physical yoga class, comparing yourself to others should be avoided, as we are all different and have different ranges.

A modification can make a challenging pose accessible, allowing you to practice safely. You will know your body best. It is absolutely fine to adapt to suit your body and its needs. The important thing is to attempt the poses and modify them as needed. If you can't get your foot up to your groin in Tree Pose, start with just lifting your foot to your ankle, or shin and work from there. If you can't get into Boat Pose and form a V, start just by lifting your heels off the floor. If you have knee or wrist pain for example, support yourself with a rolled-up towel. Or if you are using a yoga mat, roll it up to make it more supportive. You might find it works better for you by using your fists or resting on your forearms.

Vary Your Practice

Repetitive movements targeting the same muscle groups might lead to overuse injuries. To prevent this, diversify your Toothbrush Yoga practice. Explore different poses, engage various muscle groups, and challenge your body in diverse ways.

For example, if your hamstrings are sore, maybe practice a standing balance pose, instead of a Forward Fold Pose. If you have a sore back, a Child's Pose would be a good restorative pose, rather than a Cobra Pose.

By varying your practice, you ensure a holistic workout, preventing strain on specific muscles and joints, with the added benefit of keeping your practice interesting and engaging.

Pre-existing Injuries

If you have pre-existing injuries, there may be physical limitations as to what your body can and can't do. If you have a back injury, be careful about backbends, if you have a knee injury, be careful about kneeling poses. Yoga isn't rocket science, so take some medical advice if you have pre-existing conditions and be wary of poses that engage the injured area.

> *An injury invites us to explore new depths of self-care, reminding us that yoga is not just a physical practice but a holistic approach to well-being.*

Rest and Recovery

Rest is as crucial as activity in any fitness regimen. Your body needs time to recover and repair. Avoid consecutive days of intense yoga. Allow your body at least one or two days of rest per week. During rest days, you can still act upon the cues that you have built but focus on activities that promote relaxation, such as meditation or breathing. Adequate sleep also plays a pivotal role in recovery. Ensure you get the rest your body needs to rejuvenate.

It may also be that it's not possible/appropriate to strike a pose wherever you are. When I was travelling and staying in accommodation with shared bathrooms, I didn't want to be seen bent double trying to touch my forehead to my shins, some people think that's just a little odd! I had to skip the stretching part of my Toothbrush Yoga framework until such time that I was back in a private bathroom. Instead, I concentrated on mindfully brushing my teeth instead. Thankfully my elastic band was still there to remind me to do it, which is why it's important to have the visual cues there as the prompt in case your environment changes.

Stacking Toothbrush Yoga within your day-to-day rituals means that there is always a next time. You just need to build in the framework, that will promote the practice. Incorporate these principles into your Toothbrush Yoga practice, and you'll not only prevent injuries but also foster a sustainable, lifelong habit.

> *Remember, the essence of yoga lies not in how extreme your stretches are, but in how mindful, balanced, and respectful you are to your body. Enjoy your practice, respect your body's boundaries, and let the journey unfold naturally, one stretch at a time.*

Navigating the Trough of Misery: Finding Your Inner Resilience

In your journey with Toothbrush Yoga, you may encounter what psychologists call the "Trough of Misery". This is that challenging phase where your initial excitement wanes, progress feels slow, and the allure of your old routines creeps in. "Trough of Misery" is not a flaw but a feature. It's a normal part of any change process. Don't worry; you're not alone in this struggle.

It's akin to the midpoint of a marathon, where the initial adrenaline has faded, and the finish line seems distant. During this phase of your Toothbrush Yoga practice, you might find your initial zeal dampening, progress feeling sluggish, and the siren call of your old habits echoing in the distance.

It's essential to recognise this phase not as a signal of failure but as a testament to your commitment. Your initial excitement was the spark that ignited the flame of change; now, it's time to feed that flame with a different kind of fuel: resilience.

Every day is a new day, some are good, some bad. Some days I can balance better than others, sometimes I feel like I've taken a step backwards and sometimes two forward. Just take each day for what it is, there will be another tomorrow.

The beauty of Toothbrush Yoga is that the rituals you perform every day are the foundations for your habit. If you fall off the habit bus, I guarantee that the bus is still going on the same route tomorrow and the next day, they aren't going to stop at any point in your life. Try and maintain just one of the habits, I will always go back to toothbrushing. It's where my journey started, and I know without fail it happens twice a day. Even if I don't feel like touching my toes, I can simply balance.

Embrace the discomfort of the Trough of Misery, for it's in these moments that your character transforms, and your habits solidify into your identity. Just as seeds push through the soil to reach the sunlight, you, too, are growing through this phase, reaching toward the light of your goals.

Every person who ever took up yoga started from a low base and didn't know whether they were doing it right!

Notes

Chapter 13: Conclusion — Embrace Toothbrush Yoga, Transform Your Life

By consciously deciding who you want to be and acting in alignment with that vision, you're not just changing habits; you're undergoing a profound identity shift. As you step into the shoes of your future self, Toothbrush Yoga becomes more than a framework — it becomes a pathway to embodying the best version of you. If you don't feel like a Yogi yet, that's fine, act as if you are until you feel like you are. Your actions shape your beliefs, reinforcing your identity in the process. Fake it 'til you make it!

Your identity is not set in stone. You have the power to change your beliefs about yourself. You have a choice in every moment. You can choose the identity you want to reinforce today with the habits you choose today.

This brings me to the deeper purpose of this book and the real reason habits matter. The beauty of Toothbrush Yoga lies in its simplicity. It celebrates the significance of small, consistent actions. By stacking Toothbrush Yoga poses onto existing habits, you create a ripple effect of positive change. These tiny habits, when practiced diligently, yield profound results. Toothbrush Yoga teaches that transformative shifts begin with incremental changes, demonstrating the incredible potential of consistent, mindful habits.

Central to Toothbrush Yoga is the art of cue-driven mindfulness. It revolves around recognising the cues embedded in your routines — from sipping your morning tea to popping to the toilet — and leveraging these cues to prompt yoga poses. By harnessing the power of triggers, you instil moments of mindful movement into your day. These cues become gentle reminders, guiding you toward a state of harmony between body, mind, and soul.

In this book, we've explored the profound impact that small, intentional changes can have when compounded over time by infusing Toothbrush Yoga into the fabric of your daily habits, activities as mundane as brushing your teeth, waiting for the kettle to boil, or sitting at your desk.

It's not the grand gestures or momentous decisions, but the subtle daily routines that carve the path to your future self. Remember, it's not about the complexity of the poses or the duration of your practice; it's about the intention of repetition. Yoga isn't a rigid discipline but a fluid, adaptable practice. It meets you where you are, accepting your limitations and celebrating your progress.

Everybody is an individual and every body is individual. Your journey is exactly that, it is yours and yours alone. Don't compare or contrast yourself with anyone else.

Whilst this book hasn't focussed on it, the poses, or asanas described are not merely physical postures; they are gateways to self-awareness, resilience, and tranquillity. By taking this route, you've stepped on a pathway to unite your physical body with your mind and spirit, creating harmony amid life's hustle and bustle.

Your Toothbrush Yoga habit can be used to embrace mindfulness, learn to savour each moment, and find joy in the simplicity of your breath, the stretch of your limbs, and the stillness of your mind.

Go from a human being doing yoga to a human being yoga.

Baron Baptiste

I hope this is just the beginning of your yoga journey. It will have its ebbs and flows, moments of breakthrough and times of plateau — you will at times miss the prompts and you won't want to practice it every day. None of this matters. Embrace it all. Each experience is your teacher, guiding you, and leading you deeper into the profound wisdom that resides within you.

Toothbrush Yoga merely scratches the surface of yoga as a discipline. There is a vast spectrum of yoga to be explored. You might find solace in the meditative aspects of Kundalini Yoga, the discipline of Ashtanga Yoga, or the heart-opening practice of Bhakti Yoga. Each tradition offers a unique lens through which you can explore the boundless realms of your inner self.

You never know, you might quit your job, start travelling around the world and suddenly decide that you'd like to become a yoga teacher on a Balinese island. Stranger things have happened. 🙂

With the turn of the last page, you are left not with an ending, but a new beginning — a continuation of the Toothbrush Yoga journey. With boundless gratitude and anticipation of your future path, may your life be a beautiful, ever-unfolding yoga practice, off or on the mat.

Namaste,

Rob

Yoga is the fountain of youth. You're only as young as your spine is flexible.

Bob Harper

Share Your Toothbrush Yoga Journey: Reviews and Testimonials

Dear fellow Toothbrush Yoga enthusiast,

I hope your journey into the transformative world of Toothbrush Yoga has been as awe-inspiring for you as it has been for me. Your dedication to incorporating mindfulness and movement into your daily life is truly admirable, and I want to express my heartfelt appreciation for putting your trust in the teachings of this book.

If you found Toothbrush Yoga to be a beneficial and enlightening experience, I kindly request you to consider sharing your thoughts and experiences with me and others. Your positive review on platforms like Amazon can make a profound impact on someone else's life, guiding them toward a path of wellness, balance, and self-discovery.

By sharing your authentic feedback, you not only fuel my passion for spreading the message of Toothbrush Yoga but also assist fellow readers in making an informed decision about embracing this practice. Your words have the incredible power to inspire and empower others, just as your unwavering dedication will inspire me on my own journey.

I want to express my deepest gratitude for being an integral part of the Toothbrush Yoga community.

Your support means the world to me, and I am genuinely grateful for your time, dedication, and enthusiasm. Together, let's continue to spread the light of Toothbrush Yoga and make a positive impact on the lives of many.

You can share your thoughts and feedback with me via Instagram - @toothbrushyoga. I look forward to hearing from you!

With boundless gratitude and warm wishes,

Rob

Notes

Toothbrush Yoga Pose Index

What is an Asana?	107
The Power of Breath in Yoga	108

A Note of Caution — A Guide to Yoga Safety   111

YouTube Short Video Pose Index   114

Standing Poses   117

Mountain Pose	118
Forward Fold Pose	119
Half Lift Pose	120
Chair Pose	121

Standing Balance Poses   123

Tree Pose	124
Eagle Pose	125
Dancer Pose	126

Standing Sequence Poses   127

Warrior 1 Pose	128
Warrior 2 Pose	129
Reverse Warrior Pose	130
Warrior 3 Pose	131
Extended Side Angle Pose	132
Triangle Pose	133
Low Lunge Pose	134
Crescent Lunge Pose	135

Kneeling Poses — **137**

- Tabletop Pose — 138
- Child's Pose — 139
- Cat/Cow Pose — 140
- Frog Pose — 141
- Camel Pose — 142
- Downward Dog Pose — 143
- Plank Pose — 144
- Pigeon Pose — 145

Seated Poses — **147**

- Easy Seating Pose — 148
- Seated Easy Seating Pose — 149
- Half Lotus Pose — 150
- Seated Side Bend Pose — 151
- Seated Side Twist Pose — 152
- Seated Cat/Cow Pose — 153
- Seated Forward Fold Pose — 154
- Seated Pigeon Pose — 155
- Seated Boat Pose — 156
- Seated Eagle Arms Pose — 157

Lying Poses — **159**

- Corpse Pose — 160
- Banana Pose — 161
- Knees-to-Chest Pose — 162
- Legs Up the Wall Pose — 163

Lying Twist Poses — 165

- Supine Spinal Twist Pose — 166
- Windscreen Wiper Pose — 167

Lying Core Body Poses — 169

- Boat Pose — 170

Lying Lower Body Poses — 171

- Reclining Bound Angle Pose — 172
- Happy Baby Pose — 173

Lying Back Bend Poses — 175

- Sphinx Pose — 176
- Upward Facing Dog Pose — 177
- Locust Pose — 178
- Cobra Pose — 179
- Bridge Pose — 180
- Developing Toothbrush Yoga Further — The Breath as Life Force — 181

In this comprehensive chapter, you'll find a detailed index that serves as your ultimate guide to navigating the vast landscape of poses or asanas you can choose.

The world of yoga is a smorgasbord of poses, and variations to those poses, each offering unique benefits for your body, mind, and spirit. This index by no means represents the totality of the possible yoga poses. I have selected them because I felt they were the most appropriate to kick-start your Toothbrush Yoga journey.

What is an Asana?

In the context of yoga, an asana is a physical posture or pose that is typically used for meditation, relaxation, or promoting physical and mental well-being.

The word "asana" is derived from the Sanskrit language, where "as" means "to sit" and "ana" means "with," implying a posture that one can sit in comfortably for an extended period.

Asanas are an essential part of yoga practice and are used to improve flexibility, balance, strength, and overall body awareness. They are designed not only to stretch and tone the physical body but also to stimulate the body's energy centres (chakras) and enhance the flow of life force energy (prana) within the body.

In traditional yoga philosophy, the practice of asanas is part of the broader system of yoga, which includes ethical guidelines (yamas and niyamas), breathing techniques (pranayama), concentration (dharana), meditation (dhyana), and ultimately, self-realisation (samadhi). Asanas prepare the body and mind for meditation and promote a sense of well-being by releasing physical tension and calming the mind.

There is a wide variety of asanas, ranging from simple seated poses to complex balancing postures. Each asana has specific benefits for the body and mind. The practice of yoga involves combining different asanas into sequences or routines, allowing practitioners to experience a holistic approach to physical and mental health.

You should listen to your body and avoid pushing yourself into positions that cause pain or discomfort. Yoga is a mindful and gentle practice that honours the body's limitations while encouraging growth and suppleness over time.

The asanas listed within this book are broken down into standing, kneeling, seated and lying down poses. You'll find English names, the intention of the pose, step-by-step instructions including variations to adapt or modify the pose, and cautions to be aware of. In the Appendix section, I have included the Sanskrit names for each of the poses - English/Sanskrit Pose Names.

The instructions provided within this book will act as a guide on how to come into and out of the poses, with supporting photos to show you the final pose. Take your time to understand the instructions, focus on just one pose initially, master this, and then move on to the next.

YouTube is a wonderful aid, if you want to see the poses practiced in real life, the Toothbrush Yoga Channel can be accessed at https://www.youtube.com/@ToothbrushYoga

Finally, the personal guidance of a qualified yoga teacher, whom you can ask questions and with whom you can discuss how you are feeling, is always beneficial.

The Power of Breath in Yoga

In yoga philosophy, breath is referred to as 'Prana,' the life force that sustains us. The ancient yogis believed that by controlling the breath, one could control the mind and body, paving the path to spiritual enlightenment. Breath is the bridge between the conscious and unconscious realms and harnessing it can elevate a yoga practice from mere physical exercise to a holistic, transformative experience.

In every yoga pose, the inhale and exhale have distinct roles. Inhales invite energy, expanding the body and creating space. Exhales, on the other hand, offer release, allowing you to sink deeper into the pose. Imagine inhaling as you prepare, gathering the strength and focus, and then exhaling slowly, surrendering into the pose, melting away tension and limitations.

The breath is a powerful tool to anchor your awareness in the present moment.

Eckhart Tolle

Elongating the Stretch

During your stretches, inhale to reach a little higher or further, and with the exhale, relax into the stretch. As you breathe out, visualise releasing any tightness, allowing the muscle fibres to elongate further.

Elongating the stretch in yoga is an invitation to dive deeper into the present moment, unravelling layers of tightness and finding freedom in the body.

Enhancing Twists

In twisting poses, inhale to elongate your spine, and as you exhale, gently twist deeper, using each exhale to go a little further into the stretch and wring out tension from your body. With every exhalation, imagine your body detoxifying and rejuvenating.

When we deepen our breath, we invite a sense of spaciousness and freedom into our practice, unlocking new levels of strength and tranquillity.

Softening and Surrendering

In challenging poses, especially those that require strength, exhales are your allies. As you exhale, soften your face, shoulders, and any clenched muscles. As you develop your yoga practice, you will naturally lengthen your breaths and as you do so, scan your body for tension, letting go of resistance, and feel the pose becoming more effortless. You will become more aware of your body and where tension is held in each pose, allowing you to focus in on this area immediately.

Balancing Acts

During balancing poses, focus on a steady exhale. As you breathe out, imagine your body becoming lighter, allowing you to find stability and balance. Exhales provide a sense of calm amidst the wobbles.

In balancing poses, we learn to embrace imperfection, accept wobbliness, and find stability in the midst of constant change.

The Breath-body Connection

Deepening poses with exhales is not just a physical practice but a mental and emotional one too.

Each exhale is an opportunity to release not only physical tension but also mental clutter and emotional baggage. With every breath out, let go of self-doubt, fear, and negativity, making space for self-assurance, courage, and positivity.

In the enchanting interplay of breath and yoga poses, exhales become the gateway to profound relaxation, heightened awareness, and deeper embodiment. Embrace the transformative power of your breath, and let it guide you into the heart of every pose, enriching your practice and your life.

Without the breath, there is no life. Take a moment to appreciate its presence and its gift to you.

Unknown

A Note of Caution — A Guide to Yoga Safety

Yoga is a transformative practice, but it's equally essential to ensure you transition both in and out of poses mindfully to prevent strain, especially on your back. Before delving into the suggested poses, here are some tips to protect your body during yoga.

Prenatal Yoga: Nurturing Both Body and Baby

Pregnancy is a transformative journey that brings immense joy and excitement. It is also a time when the body undergoes significant changes, both physically and mentally. If you are pregnant and embarking on a Toothbrush Yoga journey, there are prenatal yoga classes specifically designed for pregnant women which offer a gentle and nurturing way to stay active, reduce stress, and prepare for childbirth. I recommend attending these and discussing any of the suggested poses with both a healthcare professional and a pregnancy-trained yoga teacher.

Prenatal yoga is a sanctuary for expectant mothers, offering a space to reconnect with their breath, body, and baby, fostering a sense of harmony and well-being.

Engage Your Core

Maintain core engagement in all poses. A strong core supports your spine and reduces the risk of back injuries, therefore engage your abdominal muscles to stabilise your back during transitions.

Proper Alignment

Pay attention to your body's alignment. Whether you're bending forward, backwards, or twisting, keep your spine lengthened and straight. Proper alignment ensures that the force is distributed evenly across your back.

As we align our physical body in yoga, we also align our thoughts, emotions, and intentions, paving the way for holistic well-being.

Do I need Yoga Props?

Yoga props are supportive accessories used in yoga practice to help practitioners maintain proper alignment, provide stability, and enhance the overall experience of the poses. They are especially useful for beginners, individuals with limited flexibility, or those recovering from injuries. Here are some common yoga props along with household items that can act as substitutes: always ensure your makeshift props are stable and won't cause injury during your practice.

The most important pieces of equipment you need for doing yoga are your body and your mind.

Rodney Yee

While these household items can be temporary replacements for yoga props, you might want to consider investing in proper yoga props for regular practice, as they are designed to provide optimal support and safety. Leaving props in obvious places will also act as prompts to help reinforce the habits you are developing.

- **Blocks** — provide height and support, especially in poses where you need to bring the floor closer to you. Large, thick books can serve as stable substitutes, and stacking firm cushions or pillows can also create a makeshift block.
- **Straps** — assist in stretching and deepening your poses by extending your reach. A long belt or scarf can be used as a yoga strap.
- **Blankets** — provide cushioning and support in seated postures and can also be used for warmth during relaxation poses. Folded blankets or thick towels can replace yoga blankets.
- **Bolsters** — are firm pillows used to support various parts of the body, enhancing relaxation and restorative poses. Firm sofa cushions, decorative throw pillows or rolled blankets can be used as a substitute for smaller bolsters.
- **Modify poses** — don't hesitate to modify poses. If a full expression of a pose puts stress on your back, modify it. For instance, practice a half-cobra instead of a full cobra to protect your lower back during backbends.
- **Bend your knees** — when bending forward, especially in poses like Forward Fold Pose bend your knees slightly. This helps in releasing tension from your lower back and hamstrings.
- **Hip hinging** — focus on the hip hinge technique. When transitioning into poses that require forward bending, initiate the movement from your hips rather than your back. This technique protects your spine by engaging the powerful muscles of your hips.
- **Mindful exits** — exiting a pose is as crucial as entering it. Instead of abruptly coming out of a posture, reverse the movements mindfully. This controlled approach ensures that you don't strain your back muscles or ligaments. Again, engage your core to protect your back.
- **Listen to your body** — above all, listen to your body. If you feel any back pain practicing any of the poses, stop immediately. Yoga is about self-awareness and self-care. Honour your body's signals and adjust your practice accordingly. This process is about building slowly through the repetition of habitual tasks. There is no goal to attain, other than your overall well-being.

- **Counter poses** — in yoga, a counter pose, also known as a counter-stretch or counter-asana, is a posture practiced after a particular asana (yoga pose) to neutralise the body and release any tension or strain that may have been created during the preceding pose. Counter poses are used to bring the body back to a balanced and relaxed state. They serve several important purposes in yoga practice.

    This is particularly useful for neutralising the spine. Yoga sequences often involve various spinal movements such as twists, bends, and extensions. Counter poses like Child's Pose can help neutralise the spine, allowing it to return to its natural curvature after being in different positions. For example, if you have just practiced a backbend such as a Bridge Pose, a counter pose like a Knees-to-Chest Pose or a gentle forward bend such as a Forward Fold Pose can help stretch the spine in the opposite direction, relieving any compression in the spine and promoting a sense of balance.

    Using counter poses in yoga practice helps maintain a harmonious balance in the body and ensures that the practice is both effective and safe. They play a crucial role in creating a holistic and well-rounded yoga sequence.

Seek Guidance

If you're uncertain about a specific pose, seek guidance from a certified yoga teacher. They can offer personalised tips and adjustments tailored to your body's needs. You are always welcome to ask any questions on Instagram @toothbrushyoga.

By incorporating a mindful approach into your yoga practice, you not only protect your body but also enhance your overall yoga experience.

If you are struggling with any injuries, particularly around the back, it is worthwhile consulting a healthcare professional and discussing your injuries and plans. Many poses can be modified to suit your needs, ensuring a safe practice.

Remember, yoga is a journey, and each transition is an opportunity to deepen your awareness and practice self-compassion.

Through seeking guidance in yoga, we find guidance within ourselves, tapping into our intuition and deepening our connection with our own inner teacher.

YouTube Short Video Pose Index

Standing Poses

Mountain Pose	https://tinyurl.com/Mountain-Pose
Forward Fold Pose	https://tinyurl.com/ForwardFoldPose
Half Lift Pose	https://tinyurl.com/HalfLiftPose
Chair Pose	https://tinyurl.com/Chair-Pose

Standing Balance Poses

Tree Pose	https://tinyurl.com/Tree-Pose-Vrksasana
Eagle Pose	https://tinyurl.com/Eagle-Pose-Garudasan
Dancer Pose	https://tinyurl.com/DancerPose

Standing Sequence Poses

Warrior 1 Pose	https://tinyurl.com/Warrior-1
Warrior 2 Pose	https://tinyurl.com/Warrior-2
Reverse Warrior Pose	https://tinyurl.com/Reverse-Warrior
Warrior 3 Pose	https://tinyurl.com/Warrior-3
Extended Side Angle Pose	https://tinyurl.com/ExtendedSideAnglePose
Triangle Pose	https://tinyurl.com/TrianglePose
Low Lunge Pose	https://tinyurl.com/LowLungePose
Crescent Lunge Pose	https://tinyurl.com/ReverseWarriorPose

Kneeling Poses

Tabletop Pose	https://tinyurl.com/Tabletoppose
Child's Pose	https://tinyurl.com/childs-pose
Cat/Cow Pose	https://tinyurl.com/Cat-CowPose
Frog Pose	https://tinyurl.com/frogpose
Camel Pose	https://tinyurl.com/Camel-Pose
Downward Dog Pose	https://tinyurl.com/DownDogPose
Plank Pose	https://tinyurl.com/Plank-Pose
Pigeon Pose	https://tinyurl.com/PigeonPose-EkaPadaR

Seated Poses

Easy Seating Pose	https://tinyurl.com/EasySeatingPose
Seated Easy Seating Pose	https://tinyurl.com/EasySeatingPose
Half Lotus Pose	https://tinyurl.com/Half-Lotus-Pose
Seated Side Bend Pose	https://tinyurl.com/SeatedSideBendPose
Seated Side Twist Pose	https://tinyurl.com/SeatedSideTwistPose
Seated Cat/Cow Pose	https://tinyurl.com/Cat-CowPose
Seated Forward Fold Pose	https://tinyurl.com/ForwardFoldPose
Seated Pigeon Pose	https://tinyurl.com/PigeonPose-EkaPadaR
Seated Boat Pose	https://tinyurl.com/BoatPose-Navasana
Seated Eagle Arms Pose	https://tinyurl.com/Eagle-Pose-Garudasan

Lying Poses

Corpse Pose	https://tinyurl.com/CorpsePose-Savasana
Banana Pose	https://tinyurl.com/BananaPose-Bananasana
Knees-to-Chest Pose	https://tinyurl.com/Knees-to-ChestPose-Apanasana
Legs Up the Wall Pose	https://tinyurl.com/LegsUptheWallViparitaKarani

Lying Twist Poses

Supine Spinal Twist Pose — https://tinyurl.com/SupineSpinalTwistPose

Windscreen Wiper Pose — https://tinyurl.com/Windscreenwiperpose

Lying Core Poses

Boat Pose — https://tinyurl.com/BoatPose-Navasana

Lying Lower Body Poses

Reclining Bound Angle Pose — https://tinyurl.com/RecliningBoundAnglePose

Happy Baby Pose — https://tinyurl.com/HappyBabyPose-AnandaBalasana

Back Bend Poses

Sphinx Pose — https://tinyurl.com/SphinxPose

Upward Facing Dog Pose — https://tinyurl.com/UpDogPose

Locust Pose — https://tinyurl.com/LocustPose-Shalabhasana

Cobra Pose — https://tinyurl.com/Sphinx-Pose

Bridge Pose — https://tinyurl.com/Bridge-Pose

Standing Poses

Half Lift Pose

Half Lift Pose, (Ardha Uttanasana), is a foundational yoga posture that emphasises lengthening the spine and creating a flat back. This pose is often used as a transitional movement, promoting proper alignment, and preparing the body for more advanced standing poses.

Steps to Achieve the Pose

- Begin in Mountain Pose, place your hands on your hips to support the lower back.
- Inhale deeply, lengthening your spine and lifting your chest forward.
- Engage your core and exhale as you hinge at your hips, keeping your back flat and your gaze forward. Your torso should be parallel to the ground.
- Place your hands on your shins, fingertips on the floor, or on yoga blocks for support. Keep your back straight and avoid rounding your spine.
- Pull your shoulder blades down your back, creating a broad chest. Keep your neck in line with your spine and look forward.
- Hold the pose for 30 seconds to 1 minute, or longer if comfortable. Focus on relaxing the neck and shoulders, allowing your head to hang heavy.
- When releasing from the pose, engage the core, hinge from the hips, and use the hands on the knees to lever out.

Variations to Extend the Pose

- For a deeper stretch, you can extend your arms forward, reaching towards the floor /yoga blocks. Experiment with lifting your toes while in the pose to engage the leg muscles more intensively.

Cautions and Modifications

Individuals with lower back issues should avoid rounding the spine. Maintain a flat back and a slight bend in the knees. If you have neck problems, keep your gaze forward or slightly down to avoid straining the neck muscles.

Chair Pose

Chair Pose, (Utkatasana), embodies strength, stability, and focus. This pose intends to build strength in the legs and core, improve balance, and cultivate concentration. It challenges your muscles and encourages proper alignment, making it a valuable pose for body awareness and endurance.

Steps to Achieve the Pose

- Begin in Mountain Pose, inhale and raise arms overhead, palms facing each other. Exhale and bend your knees, as if you are sitting back into a chair. Keep your chest lifted and gaze forward.
- Ensure your knees are not extending beyond your toes. Engage your core muscles to support your lower back.
- Distribute your weight equally on both feet, pressing down through your heels and keeping your toes light, reaching through your hands. Breathe deeply and steadily. Focus on maintaining a smooth and controlled breath.
- Inhale and you stand, releasing the pose.

Variations to Extend the Pose

- Twisting Chair Pose: From Chair, twist your torso to one side, placing the opposite elbow on the outside of the bent knee. Hold the twist for a few breaths and then switch sides.
- Eagle Arms: Bring your arms to shoulder height, crossing your right arm under your left. Bend your elbows, bringing your palms together, holding this position.

Cautions and Modifications

Individuals with knee or lower back issues should be cautious and can practice a modified version by not bending the knees as deeply. If balance is a concern, practice near a wall or use a chair for support. Pregnant individuals can practice a wider stance and avoid deep bends to accommodate their changing centre of gravity.

NOTES

Standing Balance Poses

Tree Pose

Tree Pose, (Vrksasana), symbolises balance, grounding, and stability. The pose intention is to cultivate a sense of rootedness and poise, both physically and mentally. Strengthens the leg muscles, especially the calves, thighs, and glutes as well as stretching the inner thighs, groins, and chest.

Steps to Achieve the Pose

- Begin in Mountain Pose, shift your weight onto your right leg, gripping with your toes to find a stable base.
- Bend your left knee and place the sole of your left foot on the inner right thigh or calf, gently pulling backwards. Avoid placing it directly on the knee to protect the joint.
- Engage your core muscles and standing knee, keeping your pelvis in a neutral position.
- Bring your palms together in a prayer position (anjali mudra) in front of your heart.
- Find a static focal point in front of you to maintain balance, and breathe deeply and steadily, focusing on your breath to enhance your stability and concentration.
- Hold the pose for 30 seconds to 1 minute, or as long as you feel comfortable, maintaining your balance and focus.
- Release by grounding your left foot and practice on the other foot.

Variations to Extend the Pose

- As with all balance poses, to challenge yourself further, try closing your eyes.

Cautions and Modifications

Individuals with ankle or knee injuries should practice with caution. If balancing on one leg is challenging, you can place the toes of your lifted foot on the ground for support, avoiding the inner standing leg. Using a wall or a chair for support is also beneficial, especially for beginners or those working on improving balance.

Eagle Pose

Eagle Pose, (Garudasan), symbolises focus, balance, and concentration. This pose encourages mental and physical equilibrium, enhancing concentration and clarity. It also stretches the shoulders and hips, promoting flexibility and mobility in these areas. The intention is to cultivate a sense of poise, stability, and mental alertness.

Steps to Achieve the Pose

- Begin in Mountain Pose with your arms at your side.
- Shift your weight onto your right leg, gripping with your toes to find a stable base and lift your left leg, crossing it over your right thigh. If possible, hook your left foot behind your right calf.
- Extend your arms forward parallel to the ground.
- Cross your right arm over your left, bending both elbows. Bring your palms together, or if that's challenging, press the backs of your hands together.
- Ground your standing foot firmly into the floor, gripping with your toes. Engage your core muscles to maintain stability.
- Breathe deeply and steadily, finding a focal point to assist with balance and concentration.
- Hold the pose for 30 seconds to 1 minute, then slowly release and repeat on the opposite side.

Variations to Extend the Pose

- To challenge your balance further, try closing your eyes.

Cautions and Modifications

Individuals with knee or ankle injuries should be cautious. Modify the pose by keeping the toes of the lifted foot on the ground or practice the seated variation. If you have shoulder injuries, avoid forcing the arms into the full position. Keep the arms at a comfortable height or modify with an open-arm variation.

Dancer Pose

Dancer Pose, (Natarajasana), embodies grace, strength, and balance. This pose represents the cosmic dance of Lord Shiva and his divine harmony with the universe. Practicing Dancer Pose encourages focus, concentration, and the melding of physical and mental poise.

Steps to Achieve the Pose

- Begin in Mountain Pose, shift your weight onto your right leg, gripping with your toes to find a stable base.
- Bend your left knee, reach your left hand back and hold the inside of your left foot or ankle.
- Extend your right arm forward, parallel to the ground.
- Ground your standing foot firmly into the floor. Engage your core muscles to maintain stability.
- Inhale deeply, lifting your chest and reaching your left foot away from your body.
- Exhale slowly, maintaining your balance and focus.
- Hold the pose for 30 seconds to 1 minute, then slowly release your foot and repeat on the opposite side.

Variations to Extend the Pose

- Dancer Pose with a Wall: Practice the pose near a wall for support. Press your raised foot into the wall to help with balance.
- Quad Stretch Variation: From the balanced position, bring your foot closer to your glutes, intensifying the stretch in your quadriceps.

Cautions and Modifications

Beginners can practice Dancer Pose with a hand on a wall for balance. Gradually work on balance until you can practice the pose without support. If you experience discomfort in your hip flexors, modify the pose by not lifting your leg as high, focusing on the stretch rather than height.

Standing Sequence Poses

Warrior 1 Pose

Warrior 1 Pose, (Virabhadrasana I), embodies strength, stability, and focus. This foundational yoga posture symbolises the warrior spirit within., strengthening the legs, thighs, and ankles.

Steps to Achieve the Pose

- Begin in Mountain Pose, step your left foot back, keeping it about 3 to 4 feet away from your right foot. Both feet should be aligned, with your right foot pointing forward and your left foot angled slightly outward.
- Square your hips and shoulders, ground your feet into the floor, distributing your weight evenly.
- Inhale, raise your arms overhead and bring your palms together in Anjali Mudra (prayer position). Keep your shoulders relaxed, down and away from your ears.
- Engage your quadriceps and draw your tailbone down, lengthening your spine.
- Press your back heel into the floor, ensuring your left leg has a slight bend.
- Inhale deeply, expanding your chest and lifting your gaze slightly upward.
- Exhale slowly, maintaining the strength in your legs and the lift in your chest.
- Hold the pose for 30-60 seconds, breathing steadily, and finding your focus.
- To release, exhale, lower arms, step your back foot forward, and repeat for the opposite side.

Variations to Extend the Pose

- Warrior 1 with Backbend: In Warrior 1, release your hands behind your back, interlace your fingers, and gently straighten your arms, opening your chest into a backbend.

Cautions and Modifications

If you have lower back issues, shorten your stance, or modify the pose by not bending as deeply in the front knee. Use a wall or chair for balance if you find it challenging to maintain stability. If bringing your palms together is difficult, keep your hands shoulder-width apart or place them on your hips.

Warrior 2 Pose

Warrior 2 Pose, (Virabhadrasana II), embodies strength, courage, and openness. This classic standing posture represents a warrior gazing into the distance, ready to face challenges with determination. Strengthens the legs, especially the thighs and calves.

Steps to Achieve the Pose

- Begin in Mountain Pose, step your left foot back, keeping it about 3 to 4 feet away from your right foot. Both feet should be aligned, with your right foot pointing forward and your left foot angled slightly outward. Ground your feet, ensuring your weight is evenly distributed.
- Keep your right knee bent at 90 degrees, aligning it with your right ankle, maintaining a slight bend in your left leg, with your foot slightly turned inward.
- Engage your quadriceps and draw your tailbone down, maintaining a neutral spine.
- Open your hips and shoulders to be in line as much as possible.
- Extend your arms parallel to the ground, palms facing down, forming a straight line from fingertip to fingertip and reaching actively in opposite directions. Gaze over your right fingertips.
- Relax your shoulders away from your ears and open your chest.
- Exhale slowly, sinking deeper into the lunge while maintaining the integrity of the pose.
- Hold the pose for 30 seconds to 1 minute, breathing steadily and focusing on the strength and stability of a warrior.
- To release, exhale, lower arms, step your back foot forward, and repeat for the opposite side.

Cautions and Modifications

If you have knee issues, reduce the depth of your lunge, or practice the pose with your back against a wall for support. Use a chair or a block under your front hand for balance if needed. If gazing over your fingertips strains your neck, look straight ahead or down to the floor.

Reverse Warrior Pose

Reverse Warrior Pose, (Viparita Virabhadrasana), is a grounding and expansive posture that focuses on opening the side body while maintaining a strong foundation. Stretches and strengthens the legs, particularly the thighs and calves, and provides a deep stretch to the side body, enhancing flexibility in the spine and ribcage.

Steps to Achieve the Pose

- Begin in Warrior 2 Pose, turn your front hand over so your palm faces upwards.
- Maintain a strong foundation with your feet firmly rooted into the ground.
- Inhale and lift your right arm towards the ceiling, keeping it in line with your ear.
- As you exhale, gently slide your left hand down your back leg, reaching towards your left ankle.
- Keep your chest open and facing forward. Look up at your right hand if it feels comfortable for your neck.
- Hold the pose for several breaths, maintaining a steady flow of breath.
- To release, exhale, lower your arms, step your back foot forward, and repeat for the opposite side.

Variations to Extend the Pose

- For a deeper stretch, try reaching your left hand further down your leg or place your left hand on the ground behind your back foot.

Cautions and Modifications

If you have neck or shoulder issues, avoid looking up and keep your gaze straight ahead. Individuals with lower back problems can modify the pose by placing a hand on a block or the back of a chair.

Warrior 3 Pose

Warrior 3 Pose, (Virabhadrasana III), embodies balance, focus, and stability. This pose symbolises the warrior's courage and determination, requiring strength and concentration. Strengthens the legs, especially the thighs, hamstrings, and calves, and activates the core muscles.

Steps to Achieve the Pose

- Begin in Mountain Pose, shift your weight onto your right leg and slightly lift your left foot off the ground, finding your balance. Engage your core muscles to maintain stability.
- Extend your arms, parallel to the ground, with palms facing each other.
- Keep your hips square and maintain a micro-bend in your actively engaged standing knee.
- Straighten your left leg behind you, keeping it in line with your body.
- Press firmly into your right foot, gripping with your toes to find a stable base. Flex your left foot, pointing your toes toward the floor. Aim for a straight line from your head to your left heel.
- Maintain a neutral spine, avoiding arching or rounding your back.
- Find a focal point on the floor to help with balance and concentration.
- Breathe deeply, expanding your chest, and maintain steady breathing.
- Hold the pose for 30 to 60 seconds, focusing on your alignment and breath.
- To release, gently lower your left leg, and return to Mountain Pose.

Variations to Extend the Pose

- Half Warrior 3: If full Warrior 3 is challenging, practice with your hands on a block or the back of a chair for support.

Cautions and Modifications

Use a wall or a chair for balance support, especially if you're a beginner. If you have back issues, avoid arching your spine excessively; focus on maintaining a neutral back.

Extended Side Angle Pose

Extended Side Angle Pose, (Utthita Parsvakonasana), is a powerful standing asana that enhances strength, flexibility, and balance. This pose cultivates stability and openness in the legs and hips while stretching the side body. Strengthens and tones the legs, especially the quadriceps and inner thighs.

Steps to Achieve the Pose

- Begin in Warrior 2 Pose, reach down with your front hand to your front leg.
- Rotate your back arm around towards the floor and over your head in line with your back leg.
- Tilt your pelvis slightly forward, engaging your core muscles to maintain stability.
- Press firmly into both feet, feeling a connection with the ground.
- Keep your torso open and your chest lifted. Gaze upwards if it feels comfortable for your neck.
- Inhale deeply, expanding your chest and maintaining a steady breath.
- Exhale slowly, allowing your body to sink deeper into the pose.
- Hold the pose for 30 seconds to 1 minute, focusing on your breath and alignment of your body.
- To release, inhale as you straighten your right knee and return to the starting position.
- Repeat on the other side.

Variations to Extend the Pose

- Bound Extended Side Angle Pose: Reach your bottom arm behind your back and clasp your fingers, creating a bind that opens the chest and shoulders further.

Cautions and Modifications

If you have knee issues, reduce the depth of your right bend or practice against a wall for support. If you feel strain in your hip flexors, widen your stance or lessen the depth of your lunge. To protect your lower back, engage your core muscles and avoid overarching your spine. Use a block under your bottom hand or practice near a wall to enhance balance.

Triangle Pose

Triangle Pose, (Utthita Trikonasana), intends to create a sense of openness and lengthening in the spine, strengthening the legs and core muscles while stretching the hips and hamstrings.

Steps to Achieve the Pose

- Begin in Mountain Pose, step your feet wide apart, approximately 3 to 4 feet, depending on your comfort and flexibility.
- Turn your right foot out 90 degrees and pivot your left foot slightly inward, with your heel aligned.
- Engage your core and quadriceps, providing stability to your legs.
- Extend your arms parallel to the ground and lengthen your torso over your right leg, reaching your right hand down to your shin, ankle, or the floor (depending on your flexibility).
- Extend your left arm upward, aligning it with your shoulders, creating a straight line from your left heel to your fingertips, gaze at your left thumb, and look straight ahead or down.
- Inhale deeply, expanding your chest and maintaining a steady breath.
- Exhale slowly, allowing your body to deepen into the stretch.
- Hold for 30 to 60 seconds, breathing deeply, and maintaining proper alignment.
- To release, inhale as you engage your core muscles and come back to the starting position, then repeat on the other side.

Variations to Extend the Pose

- Revolved Extended Triangle Pose: Twist your torso, reaching down with the opposite hand and open your chest toward the sky, extending your top arm vertically.

Cautions and Modifications

To protect your lower back, engage your core muscles and avoid collapsing your chest forward. If you experience neck discomfort, look straight ahead or down, avoiding excessive strain on your neck muscles. Use a block under your bottom hand or practice near a wall for support.

Low Lunge Pose

Low Lunge Pose, (Anjaneyasana), is a dynamic yoga posture that focuses on stretching and opening the hip flexors, quadriceps, and chest. The intention behind this pose is to create a sense of grounding, stability, and balance while encouraging deep hip opening and mindful breathing.

Steps to Achieve the Pose

- Begin in a kneeling position, your hands shoulder-width apart and your feet hip-width apart.
- Step your right foot forward between your hands, placing it near the right thumb in a kneeling position, aligning your right knee directly above your right ankle.
- Maintaining a gentle stretch in the left hip flexor, extend your leg behind you with the top of your foot on the floor.
- Engage your core muscles to stabilise your spine and balance yourself with your hands.
- Sink your hips toward the floor, feeling a deep stretch in your left hip and thigh.
- Keep your neck in line with your spine, gazing forward and touching palms overhead.
- Inhale deeply, expanding your chest and filling your lungs.
- Exhale slowly, allowing your body to sink deeper into the stretch.
- Hold the pose for 30 seconds to 1 minute, breathing steadily and consciously.
- To release, bring your hands to the floor and move back to kneeling. Repeat on the other side.

Cautions and Modifications

Place a folded blanket or cushion under your back knee for additional support and cushioning. Keep your spine straight and avoid overarching your lower back. Engage your core muscles to protect your lower back. Use yoga blocks under your hands for added support and stability, especially if you have difficulty reaching the ground.

Crescent Lunge Pose

Crescent Lunge Pose, (Anjaneyasana), is a powerful yoga posture that aims to energise the body and mind. The intention behind this pose is to build strength and stability in the legs while stretching the hip flexors, thighs, and chest.

Steps to Achieve the Pose

- Begin in a standing position Mountain Pose.
- Inhale and step your right foot back into a lunge, keeping your left knee above your left ankle.
- Ensure your back leg is straight and strong, with the ball of your right foot on the floor.
- Engage your core muscles to stabilise your spine.
- Reach your arms overhead, keeping them parallel to each other with palms facing each other or bringing your palms together in a prayer position.
- Inhale deeply, expanding your chest and reaching your arms toward the sky.
- Exhale slowly, grounding your feet and maintaining your balance.
- Hold the pose for 30 to 60 seconds, breathing steadily and consciously.
- To release, exhale and gently step your right foot forward to meet your left foot, returning to Mountain Pose, repeat on the other side.

Variations to Extend the Pose

- Twisted Crescent Lunge: Place your left elbow on the outside of your right knee, twisting your torso to the right. Extend your right arm upward, looking toward the ceiling.

Cautions and Modifications

If you have knee issues, place a folded blanket or cushion under your back knee for support. Use yoga blocks under your hands for added stability, especially if reaching the ground is challenging. Engage your core muscles and maintain a neutral spine to avoid overarching your lower back.

NOTES

Kneeling Poses

Tabletop Pose

Tabletop Pose, (Bharmanasana), is a foundational yoga pose that serves as a gateway to various movements and sequences. In this pose, your body forms a tabletop position with your hands and knees on the ground, creating a stable foundation for exploration. It promotes a neutral spine, enhancing alignment and reducing strain on the back.

Steps to Achieve the Pose

- Start on your hands and knees with wrists aligned under your shoulders and knees under your hips.
- Spread your fingers wide, grounding them firmly into the floor for stability.
- Maintain a flat back, ensuring your spine is in a neutral position.
- Keep your gaze down, neck in line with the spine.
- Engage your core muscles and breathe deeply, finding stability in the pose.

Cautions and Modifications

If you have wrist issues, consider using yoga props like wrist supports. Place a blanket or cushion under your knees for added comfort if you experience discomfort.

Child's Pose

Child's Pose, (Balasana), is a restful and calming yoga posture that promotes relaxation, stretches the spine, hips, and thighs, and gently opens the shoulders. It opens up the hips and stretches the hip flexors, promoting flexibility.

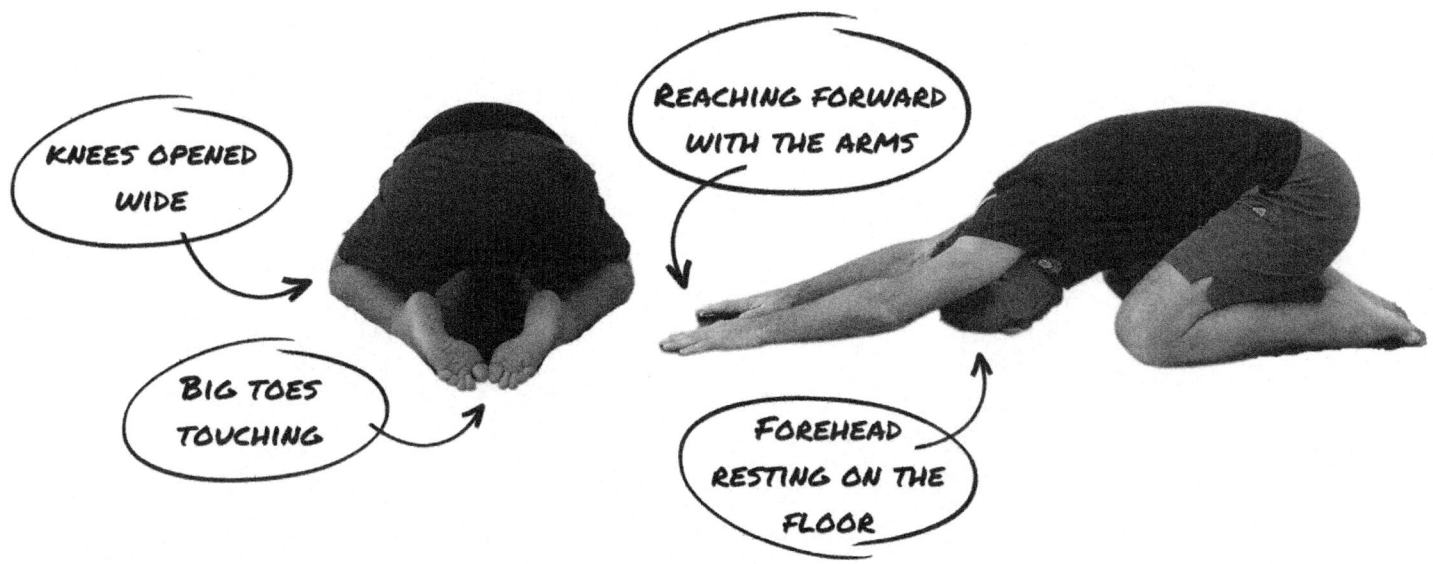

Steps to Achieve the Pose

- Begin on your hands and knees in Tabletop Pose, with your wrists aligned under your shoulders and knees under your hips.
- Spread your knees apart while keeping your big toes touching. Sit back on your heels.
- Inhale deeply, lengthening your spine.
- Exhale and slowly lower your torso down between your thighs. Your forehead should come to rest on the floor/bed.
- Extend your arms in front of you, placing your palms flat, or relax your arms by your sides with palms facing up.
- Close your eyes and focus on your breath. Hold the pose for 30 seconds to several minutes, breathing deeply and allowing your body to relax.
- To release, gently walk your hands back toward your body, lifting your torso back into a seated position.

Variations to Extend the Pose

- Wide-Arm Child's Pose: Extend your arms further out to the sides to feel a stretch in your shoulders and upper back.

Cautions and Modifications

If you have knee or ankle injuries, place a folded blanket or cushion between your thighs and calves for added support. If you have back pain, widen your knees to reduce pressure on your lower back. Individuals with high blood pressure or dizziness should avoid lowering their head below the heart level. Use a cushion under your forehead to elevate your head slightly.

Cat/Cow Pose

Cat/Cow Pose, (Marjaryasana/Bitilasana), is a gentle flow between two poses that warms the body and brings flexibility to the spine. It's a part of many yoga sequences and is great for beginners to learn the basics of spinal flexibility and alignment.

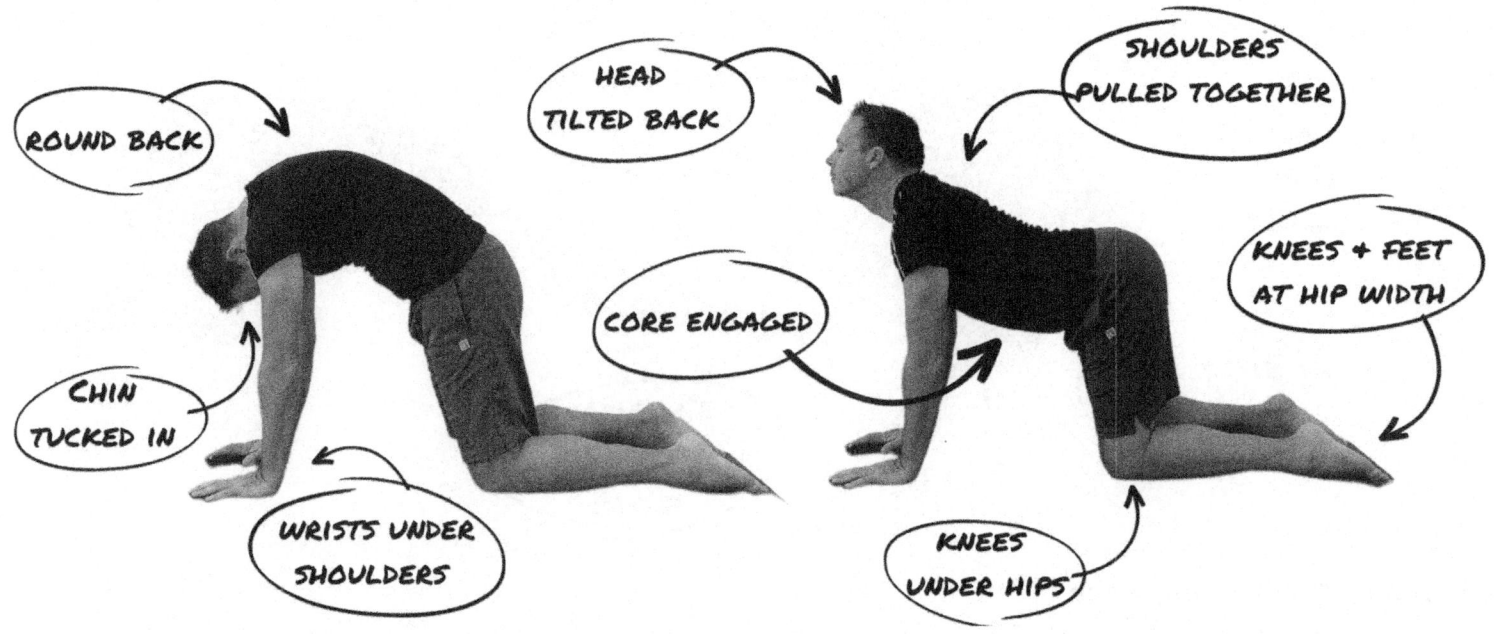

Steps to Achieve the Pose

- Begin on your hands and knees in Tabletop Pose, with your wrists aligned under your shoulders and knees under your hips.
- Engage your core, pulling your navel towards the spine, and inhale as you arch your back, pulling shoulders together, and dropping your belly towards the floor. Lift your head and tailbone towards the ceiling, creating a concave curve in your back.
- Exhale as you round your spine upwards, tucking your chin to your chest. Imagine pulling your belly button towards your spine, creating a hump in your back.
- Flow smoothly between Cat and Cow Poses, syncing your breath with the movement. Inhale into Cow Pose, and exhale into Cat Pose. Continue this gentle, flowing sequence for several breaths, focusing on the fluidity of the movement and the stretch in your spine.

Variations to Extend the Pose

- Extended Cat Pose: From the Cat Pose, extend one arm forward and the opposite leg backward, balancing on the remaining hand and knee. Hold briefly and then switch sides.
- Dynamic Cat/Cow: Add dynamic movements by incorporating side stretches or gentle twists while transitioning between Cat and Cow Poses.

Cautions and Modifications

If you experience discomfort in your wrists, place a folded towel under your wrists for support. If your knees are sensitive, practice this pose on a folded blanket for extra cushioning. If you have neck injuries, keep your head in line with your spine and avoid excessive neck movements during the poses.

Frog Pose

Frog Pose, (Mandukasana), posture resembles the position of a frog, with your legs splayed wide apart and your torso lowered towards the ground, gravity is bearing down on you opening your hips with a deep stretch. As you settle into this pose, you'll experience a deep stretch in your thighs, groins, and chest, fostering a sense of inner calm and strength.

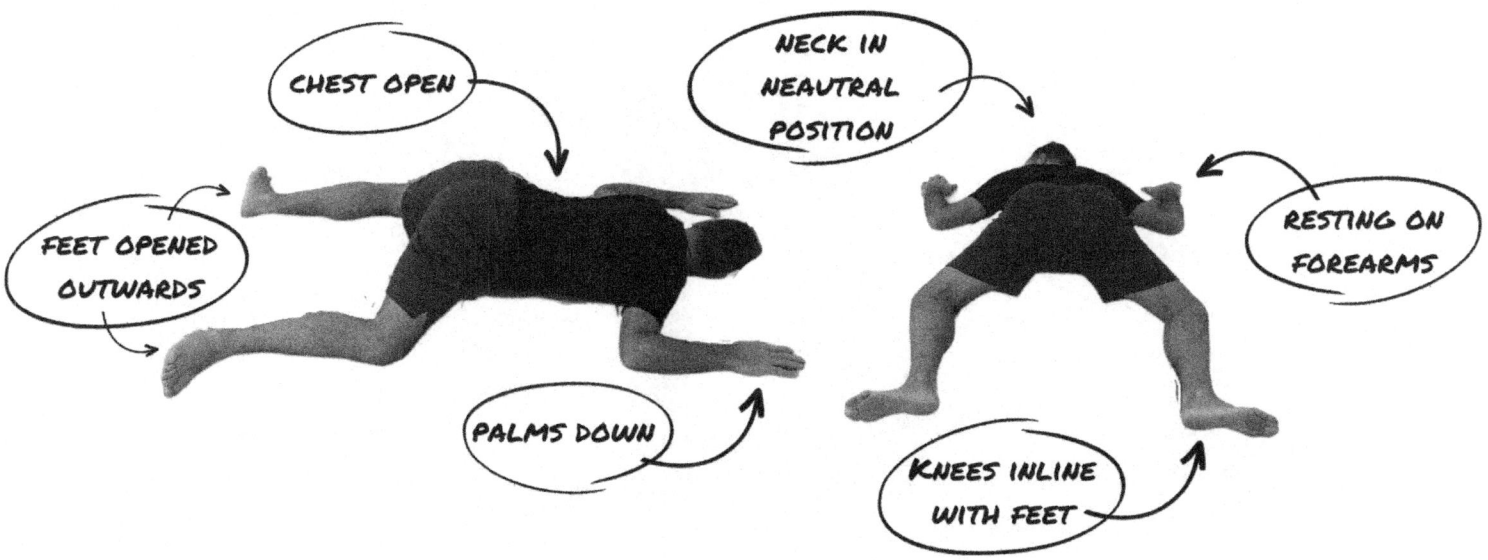

Steps to Achieve the Pose

- Begin on your hands and knees in Tabletop Pose, with your wrists aligned under your shoulders and knees under your hips.
- Gradually widen your knees apart as far as comfortable, keeping your feet in line with your knees. Your thighs should be parallel to each other, and your shins should be perpendicular to the floor. Ensure your ankles are in line with your knees, forming a right angle with your lower legs. Keep your feet flexed to protect your knees.
- Slowly lower your chest towards the ground, finding a comfortable stretch in your groins and thighs. You can rest on your forearms or extend your arms, keeping your elbows off the ground.
- Avoid arching your lower back by having your hips higher than your chest, use your forearms to support a straight spine. Keep your neck in a neutral position, lengthening your spine, and engaging your core muscles. Relax your shoulders away from your ears, opening your chest.
- Take slow, deep breaths, allowing the stretch to deepen with each exhale. Stay in the pose for 30 seconds to 5 minutes, depending on your available time, gradually increasing the duration as your flexibility improves.
- To release from the pose, come back into the Tabletop position.

Cautions and Modifications

If you find it challenging to lower your chest to the ground, place a cushion or yoga block under your chest for support. Listen to your body and avoid forcing yourself into a deep stretch. Gradually work on increasing your flexibility over time. To deepen the stretch, gently press your hips back and down while keeping your chest open and forward.

Camel Pose

Camel Pose, (Ustrasana), is a deep backbend that aims to open the chest, stretch the front of the body, and improve spinal flexibility. This pose is practiced to enhance posture, strengthen the back and thighs, as well as stretching the front of the entire body.

Steps to Achieve the Pose

- Begin on your hands and knees in Tabletop Pose, sit back on your heels with your feet and knees hip-width apart, hands on your thighs.
- Come into a kneeling position, placing your hands on your lower back.
- Inhale and engage your thighs and glutes, pressing your hips forward. Exhale and begin to arch your back.
- When your movement stops, reach your hands back, rotating your elbows inwards, one at a time, to find your heels. This can be challenging at first.
- If reaching your heels is challenging, you can keep your hands on your lower back for support or place them on the back of your thighs.
- Once your hands are on your heels, gently tilt your head back and gaze up, opening your chest.
- Hold the pose for several breaths, breathing deeply and maintaining the arch in your back.
- To release, bring your hands back to your hips, engage your core, and slowly come back to an upright position.

Variations to Extend the Pose

- Head to the Floor: For a much more advanced variation, if your back allows, you can lower your head to the floor behind you, deepening the backbend further.

Cautions and Modifications

If you have lower back issues, practice this pose with caution. Consider placing a cushion or folded blanket under your knees for support or practice a gentler variation. If you have neck injuries, avoid dropping your head back. Keep your neck in a neutral position or gaze forward.

Downward Dog Pose

Downward Dog Pose, (Adho Mukha Svanasana), embodies strength, lengthening, and grounding. This pose intends to build upper body strength, lengthen the spine, and stretch the entire back body.

Steps to Achieve the Pose

- Begin on your hands and knees in Tabletop Pose. Align your wrists under your shoulders and knees under your hips, spread your fingers wide apart, pressing firmly with your palms.
- Tuck your toes under and lift your hips toward the ceiling, straightening your legs and forming an inverted V-shape with your body. Engage core.
- Keep your head between your arms, ears aligned with your biceps, and gaze toward your navel.
- Maintain an active engagement in your arms, pushing away from you.
- Press your heels toward the floor, stretching your legs and pulling backwards with your knees, whilst keeping a slight bend in your knees if needed.
- Breathe deeply and steadily, focusing on expanding your chest and relaxing your neck and shoulders.
- Hold the pose for 30 seconds to 1 minute, focusing on deep breathing and elongating your spine.

Variations to Extend the Pose

- Downward Dog Foot Pedal: Alternate lifting and pressing down feet in a pedalling motion.
- Three-Legged Downward Dog: Lift one leg toward the ceiling, extending it straight back while keeping the hips square for Three-Legged Downward Dog.

Cautions and Modifications

Individuals with wrist, shoulder, or back injuries should practice with caution. Modify by using yoga blocks under your hands or practicing on your forearms. If your hamstrings are tight, keep a slight bend in your knees to avoid straining your lower back. For beginners, practice against a wall to focus on alignment and gradually build strength.

Plank Pose

Plank Pose, (Phalakasana), is a fundamental yoga pose designed to build strength in the entire body, especially in the core, arms, shoulders, and back. This pose intends to develop stability, improve posture, and enhance overall body awareness.

Steps to Achieve the Pose

- Begin on your hands and knees in Tabletop Pose, moving into a push-up position, step your feet back, your hands shoulder-width apart.
- Align your wrists directly under your shoulders and extend your legs straight back, creating a straight line from your head to your heels.
- Engage your core muscles and keep your body in a straight, neutral position.
- Inhale deeply, drawing your abdominal muscles in and maintaining a straight-line head to heels.
- Hold the position, keeping your gaze slightly forward and down, without collapsing your chest or lifting your hips too high. Distribute your weight evenly between your hands and toes.
- Keep your neck in line with your spine and breathe steadily, holding the pose for as long as comfortable, breathe evenly and hold the pose for as long as you feel able.
- To come out, place your knees on the floor one at a time.

Variations to Extend the Pose

- Dolphin Plank: Lower your forearms, keeping your elbows directly under your shoulders. Maintain a straight line from your head to your heels, engaging your core and leg muscles.
- Side Plank (Vasisthasana): Shift your weight to one hand and rotate your body, stacking one foot on top of the other. Raise your opposite arm toward the sky, balancing on the outer edge of your foot and hand.

Cautions and Modifications

Individuals with wrist issues can practice the pose on their forearms, known as Dolphin Plank, to reduce pressure on the wrists. If you have lower back problems, engage your core muscles more actively to maintain a straight back and avoid sagging in the lower spine. Carpal Tunnel sufferers may wish to use blocks or pillows under their hands.

Pigeon Pose

Pigeon Pose, (Eka Pada Rajakapotasana), is a deeply calming hip opener that stretches the thighs, groins, and psoas. It is practiced to release tension in the hips, increase hip flexibility, and alleviate lower back pain.

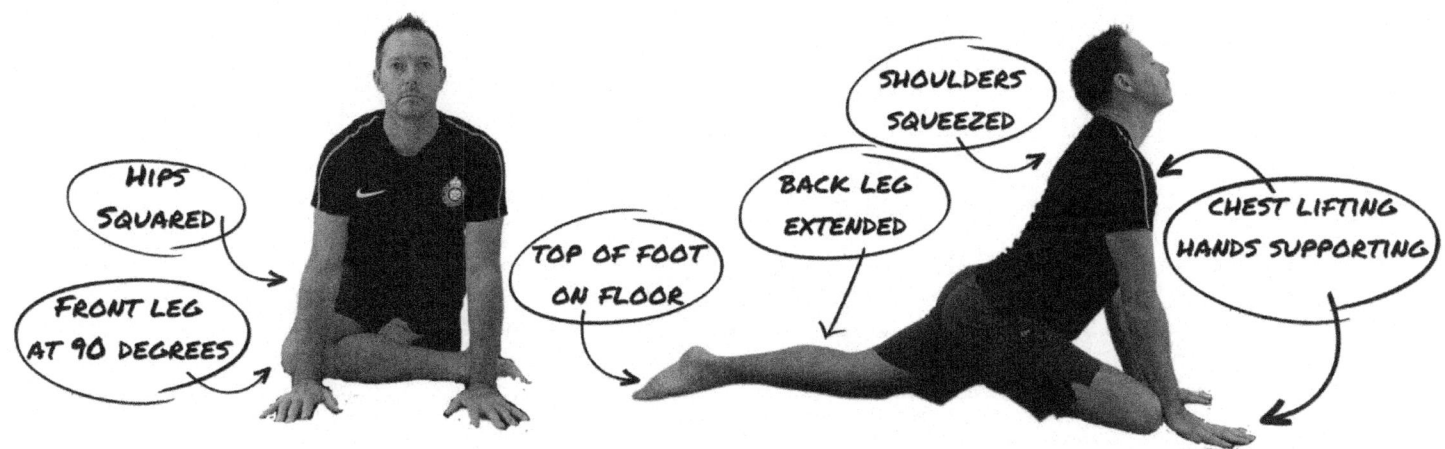

Steps to Achieve the Pose

- Begin in the Tabletop Pose and slide your right knee forward toward your right wrist. Your right ankle should be in front of your left hip, as close to 90 degrees as possible.
- Extend your left leg straight back, keeping your hips square.
- Inhale as you lengthen your spine, lifting your chest. You can stay upright or, if comfortable, begin to walk your hands forward, lowering your chest.
- Exhale and relax into the pose, allowing your hips to sink down.
- Ensure your hips are level; you can use a folded blanket or cushion under your right hip and/or extended knee for support if needed.
- Stay in the pose for 30-120 seconds, breathing deeply and relaxing into the stretch. Keep your neck in a neutral position.
- To come out of the pose, engage your core muscles, press into your hands, and lift your chest. Slide your right knee back, return to the tabletop position and then repeat on the other side.

Variations to Extend the Pose

- Pigeon Pose Twist: From the Pigeon Pose position, place your right hand in front of you. Inhale as you lift your left arm toward the ceiling, twisting gently to the right. Hold for a few breaths, then switch sides.
- King Pigeon Pose: For a deeper stretch, bend your left knee, reach back with your left hand, and hold your left foot. This variation requires significant flexibility in the shoulders and quads.

Cautions and Modifications

If you experience discomfort in your front knee, place a folded blanket or cushion under your right hip and outstretched knee for support. If you have lower back issues, avoid folding forward too deeply. Keep the pose more upright and focus on opening the hips gently. If you have neck issues, keep your head in a neutral position without looking up or down.

NOTES

Seated Poses

Easy Seating Pose

Easy Seating Pose, (Sukhasana), focuses on grounding and calming the body and mind. It aims to create a sense of ease and tranquillity, making it an excellent pose for meditation and pranayama practices. The pose gently opens the hips and stretches the knees and ankles.

Steps to Achieve the Pose

- Sit with your legs extended straight in front of you.
- Cross your legs at the shins, bringing your feet under the opposite knee.
- Place your hands on your knees, palms facing up or down.
- Find a neutral hip position by rocking gently forwards and backwards.
- Lengthen your spine, keeping your shoulders back and down. Align your head with the spine, chin slightly lowered to the chest.
- Breathe naturally, focusing on the inhales and exhales, allowing your body to relax into the pose.
- Relax your facial muscles and jaw, and close your eyes, bringing your awareness inward.
- Sit in this posture, being aware of your breath and sensations, cultivating a sense of inner peace.

Variations to Enhance the Pose

- Supported Easy Sitting Pose: Sit on a block/cushion to elevate your hips slightly, reducing knee strain and promoting a more comfortable seated position.
- Widened Legs: Draw the knees away from each other so both calves are grounded.

Cautions and Modifications

If you experience discomfort in your knees, sit on a cushion or bolster to reduce pressure on the joints. Pregnant individuals can modify Sukhasana by placing a cushion under their hips, allowing space for the belly, and ensuring comfort during the practice.

Seated Easy Seating Pose

Seated Easy Seating Pose, focuses on grounding and calming the body and mind. It aims to create a sense of ease and tranquillity, making it an excellent pose for meditation and pranayama practices. The pose gently opens the hips and stretches the knees and ankles, enhancing flexibility in these areas.

Steps to Achieve the Pose

- Sit comfortably on a chair, knee, and feet hip-width apart.
- Place your hands on your knees, palms facing up or down, in a gesture of openness or grounding.
- Find a neutral hip position by rocking gently forwards and backwards.
- Lengthen your spine, keeping your shoulders back and down. Align your head with the spine, chin slightly lowered to the chest.
- Breathe naturally, focusing on the inhales and exhales, allowing your body to relax into the pose.
- Soften your gaze or close your eyes, bringing your awareness inward. Relax your facial muscles and jaw.
- Sit in this posture, being aware of your breath and sensations, cultivating a sense of inner peace.

Half Lotus Pose

Half Lotus Pose, (Ardha Padmasana), is a classic yoga pose that is often used for meditation and breathing exercises. Practicing Half Lotus Pose regularly helps in opening the hips and increasing flexibility in the hip joints, whilst aligning the spine and improving overall body posture.

Steps to Achieve the Pose

- Begin by sitting in Easy Seating Pose.
- Bend your right knee and place the right ankle on top of the left thigh.
- Rest your hands on your knees in chin mudra (thumb and index finger touching) or gyana mudra (thumb and index finger forming a circle).
- Sit with your spine erect and shoulders relaxed, allowing your knees to rest comfortably.
- Breathe deeply and maintain the posture for the desired duration, focusing on your breath and keeping your mind calm and still.
- Switch over the feet regularly.

Variations to Extend the Pose

- If you have the flexibility, the full Lotus Pose, (Padmasana), is a challenging variation, where both feet rest on the opposite thigh and the knees rest on the floor.

Cautions and Modifications

If you experience discomfort in your knees, avoid forcing your knees down. If you feel strain in your ankles, consider placing a cushion or folded blanket under your ankles for added support. Individuals with limited hip mobility should approach Half Lotus Pose with caution. Regular hip-opening exercises can help improve flexibility over time.

Seated Side Bend Pose

The Seated Side Bend Pose focuses on stretching and lengthening the sides of your torso. It promotes lateral flexibility, allowing for better breathing and improved posture. This pose aims to release tension in the back and sides, creating a sense of openness and balance in the body.

Steps to Achieve the Pose

- Sit in Easy Seating Pose
- Inhale and raise your arms overhead, place your right hand on the side of the chair.
- Exhale and gently lean to your right, reaching your left hand overhead and to the side. Feel the stretch along your left side.
- Hold the stretch for a few deep breaths, feeling the expansion of the ribcage with each inhale and deepen the stretch with each exhale.
- Inhale and come back to the centre, releasing your arms and repeat on the other side.

Variations to Extend the Pose

- Place your hand on a block or cushion on the side to deepen the stretch and maintain stability.

Cautions and Modifications

If you have lower back problems, sit on a cushion to elevate your hips, and reduce strain. If you experience discomfort in your neck, keep your gaze forward or lower your head slightly to ease the stretch in the neck muscles. Pregnant individuals can practice a modified side bend by sitting with their backs against a wall for added support and stability.

Seated Side Twist Pose

The Seated Side Twist Pose is designed to stretch and release tension in the spine, shoulders, and neck. Improves spinal flexibility and mobility, whilst relieving tension in the shoulders and neck, common areas of stress.

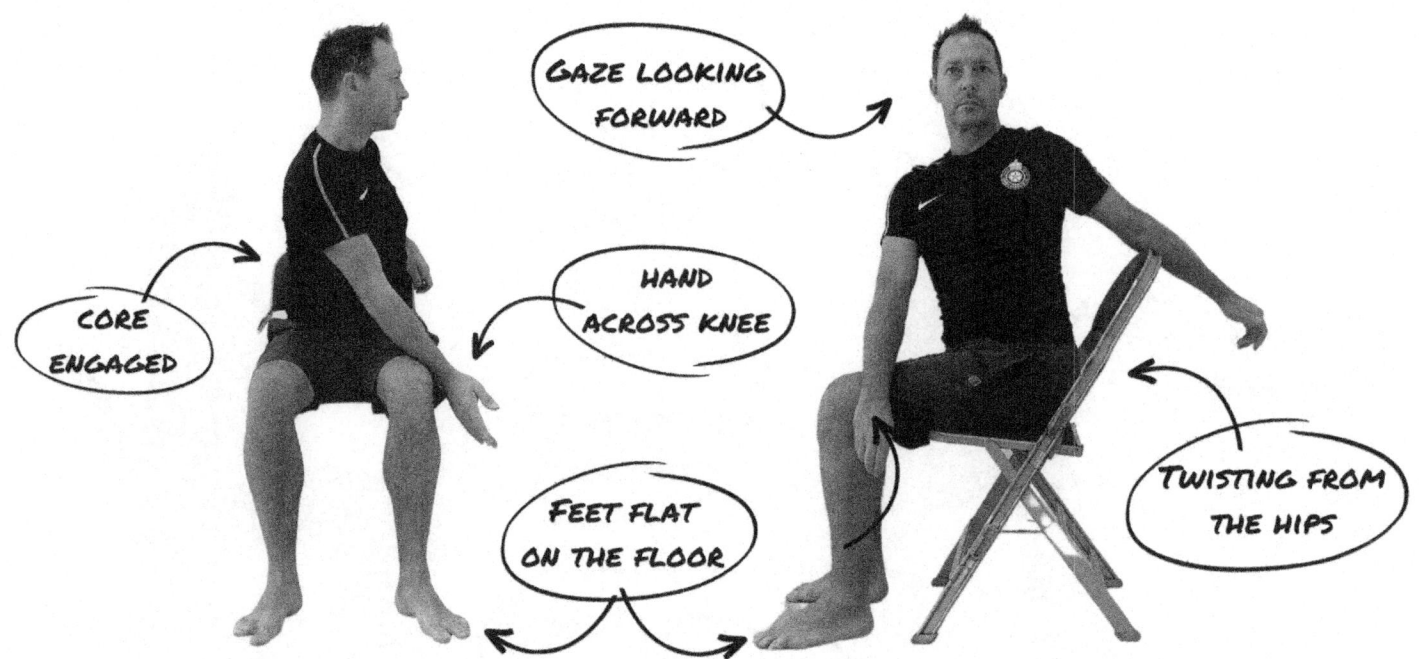

Steps to Achieve the Pose

- Sit in Easy Seating Pose
- Lifting and reaching with arms above your head, inhale deeply, elongating your spine.
- Exhale as you gently twist your torso to the left, bringing your hands downwards so your right hand is on the outside of your left knee and your left arm is resting on the chair back behind you.
- Your gaze should remain looking forward.
- Hold the twist for 20-30 seconds, breathing deeply and maintaining the length in your spine, deepen the stretch with each exhale.
- Inhale to come back to the centre.
- Repeat the twist on the opposite side by placing your left hand on your right knee and your right hand behind you.

Variations to Extend the Pose

- For a deeper twist, hook your elbow on the outside of the opposite knee, deepening the rotation.
- You can also practice this twist with your legs in a different position, such as in a half-lotus or lotus pose, to challenge your flexibility.

Cautions and Modifications

If you have back or spinal injuries, twist gently and avoid forcing your body into the pose. If sitting cross-legged is uncomfortable, sit on a folded blanket or cushion to elevate your hips. Pregnant individuals should practice this twist with caution, avoiding deep twists that compress the abdomen.

Seated Cat/Cow Pose

The Seated Cat/Cow Pose is a variation of the Cat/Cow Pose and is intended to promote spinal flexibility, improve posture, and gently stretch the back muscles.

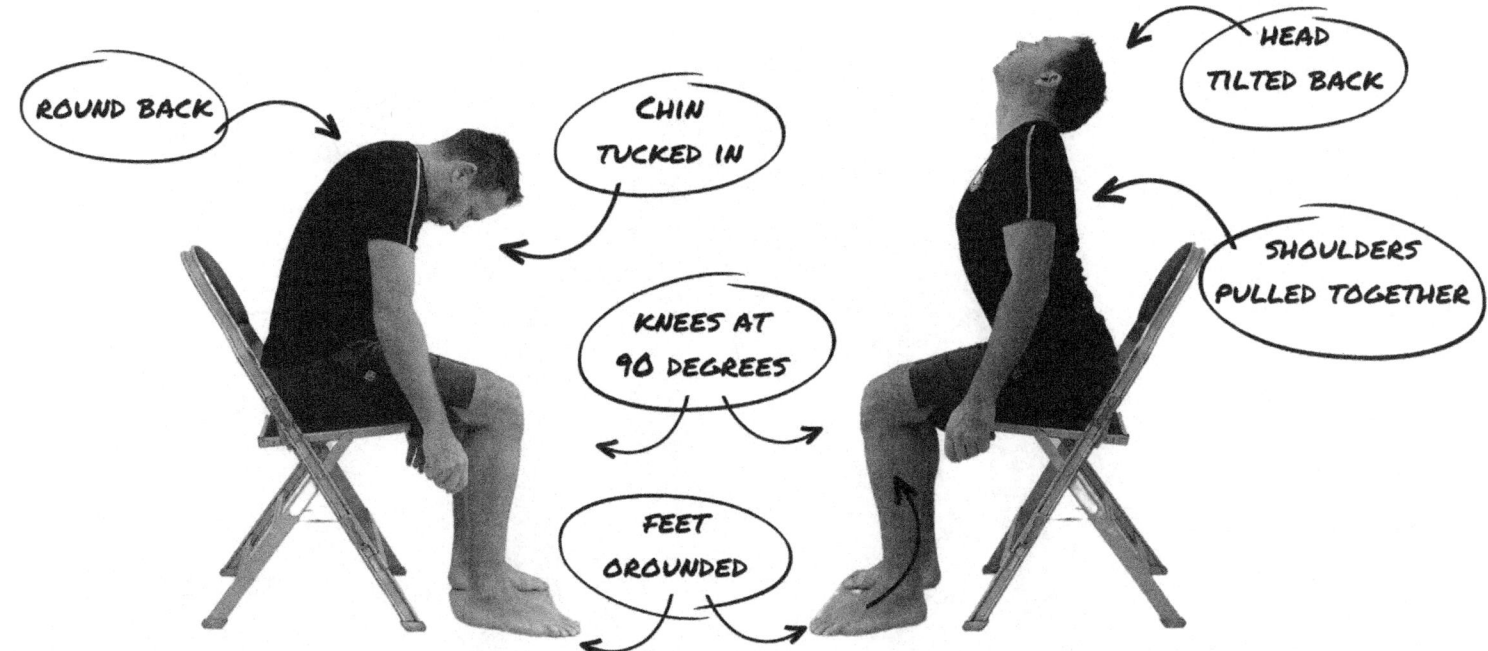

Steps to Achieve the Pose

- Sit in Easy Seating Pose and keep your shoulders relaxed and down.
- Inhale, arch your back, lift your chest and tilt your head back, creating a gentle backbend. This is the Cow Pose.
- Exhale, round your spine, tuck your chin towards your chest, and draw your belly button towards your spine, creating a C-curve in your back. This is the Cat Pose.
- Continue flowing between Cow and Cat Poses, synchronising your breath with the movement.
- Inhale during Cow Pose, and exhale during Cat Pose, allowing your breath to guide the rhythm of the movement.
- Practice this flowing motion for several rounds, focusing on the smooth articulation of your spine.

Variations to Extend the Pose

- To deepen the stretch in Cat Pose, you can engage your abdominal muscles further, drawing your belly button towards your spine and arching your back slightly.
- For a more intense backbend in Cow Pose, you can lift your arms overhead, opening your chest and reaching towards the sky.

Cautions and Modifications

Individuals with neck injuries should be cautious and avoid dropping their head too low in Cat Pose. If sitting on the chair is uncomfortable, you can place a cushion or bolster on the seat to elevate your hips slightly, making it easier to practice the movement. If there is discomfort in the wrists, you can rest your hands on the thighs and focus on the movement of the spine.

Seated Forward Fold Pose

The Seated Forward Fold Pose, a variation of the Forward Fold Pose, is designed to stretch the entire back of the body, including the spine, hamstrings, and shoulders. Improves posture and flexibility in the legs and back.

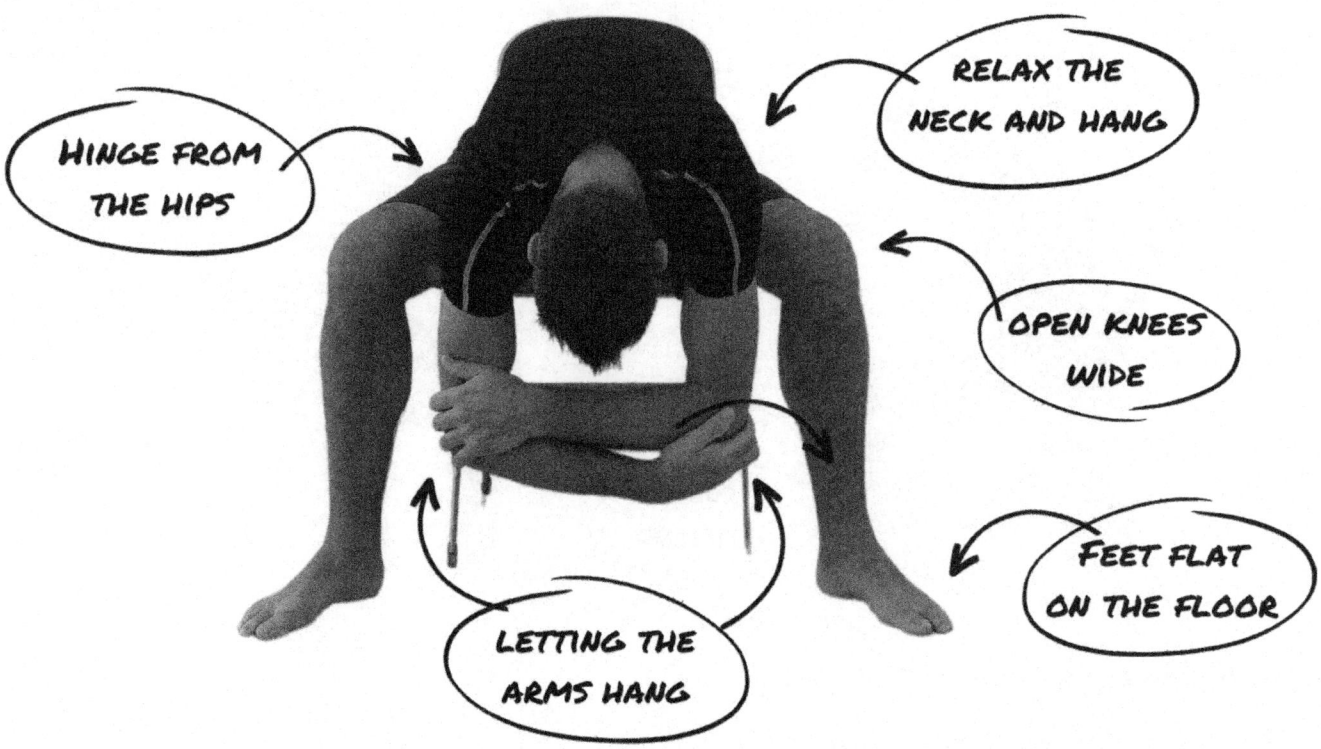

Steps to Achieve the Pose

- Sit in Easy Seating Pose
- Open your legs wide, inhale deeply, raise the arms above your head and lengthen your spine.
- Exhale slowly, hinge from your hips and lean forward between your legs.
- Place your hands on the floor, on your shins, or hold your elbows, depending on your flexibility.
- Keep your back straight as you fold forward, leading with your chest.
- Relax your neck and let your head hang heavy, allowing your spine to lengthen further.
- Hold the stretch for 30 seconds to 1 minute, breathing deeply and relaxing into the pose.

Variations to Extend the Pose

- For a deeper stretch, you can reach for your ankles, gently pulling yourself closer to your legs.
- If you have the flexibility, you can wrap a yoga strap around your feet and hold the ends, allowing your hands to slide down the strap as you deepen the stretch.

Cautions and Modifications

Individuals with lower back injuries should be cautious and may need to keep a slight bend in their knees. If reaching the floor is difficult, use yoga blocks or a stack of books to rest your hands, maintaining the integrity of the stretch. Pregnant women should separate their legs slightly to make room for the belly and avoid putting pressure on the abdomen.

Seated Pigeon Pose

The Seated Pigeon Pose, a variation of Pigeon Pose, is aimed at stretching the outer thighs, groins, and hip flexors. Stretches the outer thighs, groins, and hip flexors as well as improving hip flexibility and mobility.

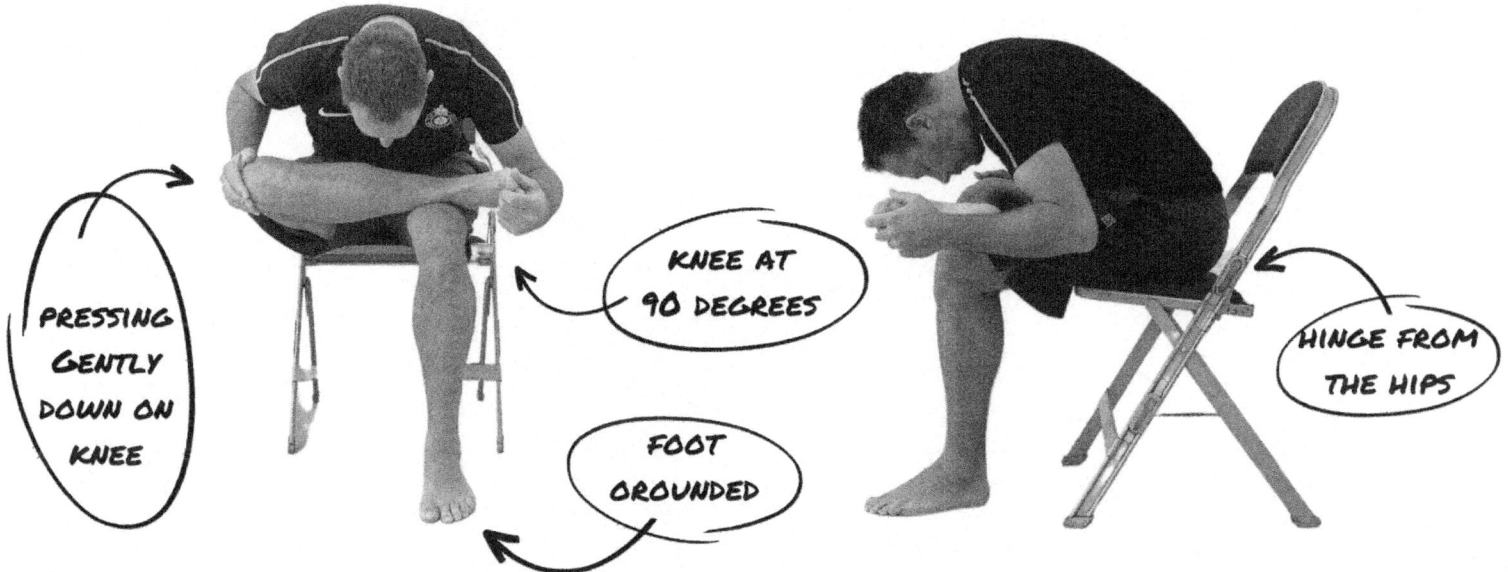

Steps to Achieve the Pose

- Sit in Easy Seating Pose
- Plant your feet flat on the ground, hip-width apart.
- Inhale deeply, lengthening your spine.
- Exhale slowly, lift your right ankle and place it on your left thigh, just above the knee.
- Flex your right foot to protect your knee and maintain the alignment.
- Press gently on your right knee to open the hip and lean forward slightly, hinging at the hips, bringing your chest closer to your thighs.
- Keep your spine straight and your chest lifted.
- Hold the stretch for 30 seconds to 1 minute, breathing deeply and relaxing into the pose.
- Repeat on the other side by placing your left ankle on your right thigh.

Cautions and Modifications

Individuals with knee injuries should be cautious and can modify the pose by not pressing the knee too hard. If sitting directly on the chair is uncomfortable, you can place a cushion or folded blanket under your hips for support. Pregnant women should avoid deep forward bends and should practice this pose with gentle modifications.

Seated Boat Pose

Seated Boat Pose is a modified version of the traditional Boat Pose and is designed to strengthen the core muscles, enhance balance, and improve posture.

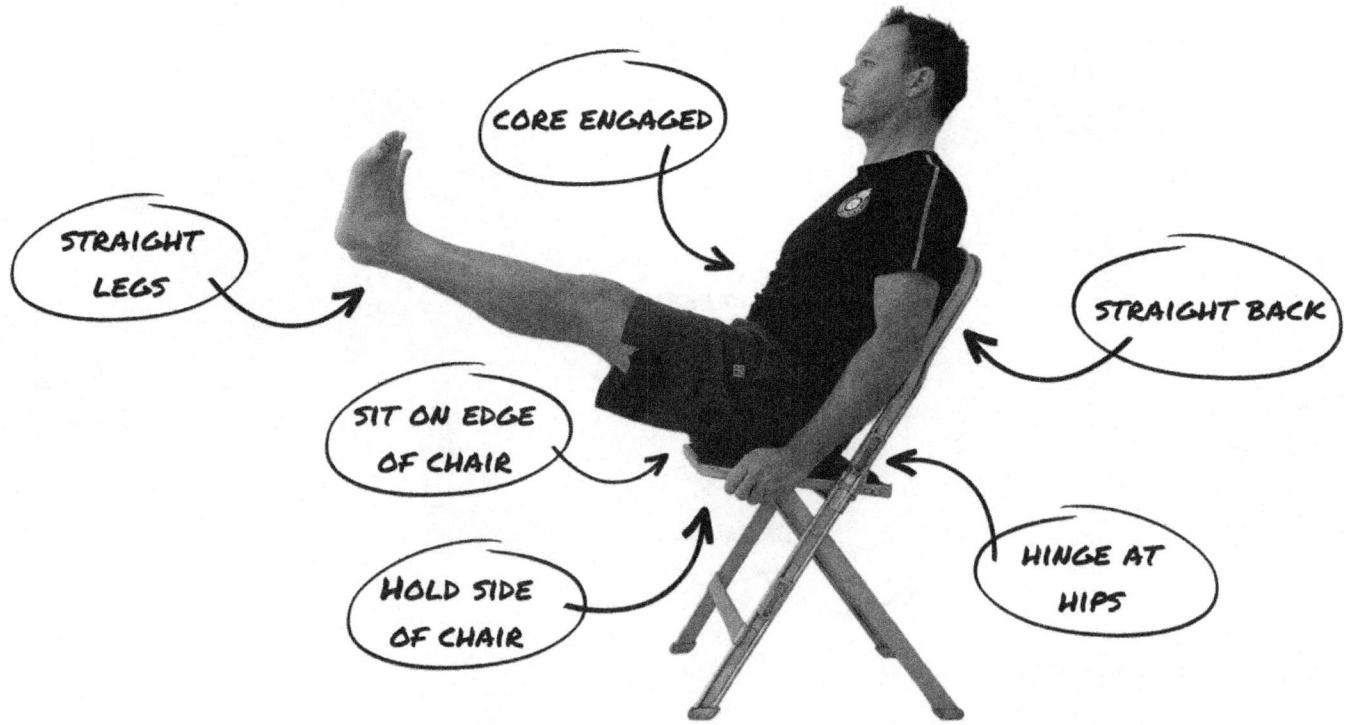

Steps to Achieve the Pose

- Sit in Easy Seating Pose
- Move to the edge of the chair with your feet flat on the ground and your spine tall.
- Place your hands on the sides of the chair, gripping the edges firmly.
- Inhale deeply, engaging your core muscles.
- Exhale, straighten your legs, and lift both feet, bringing them to parallel to the floor or above.
- Straighten your arms, keeping them parallel to the ground, holding onto the chair for support.
- Maintain a straight back and a lifted chest, engaging your abdominal muscles.
- Hold the position for 20-30 seconds, breathing steadily.
- To release, gently lower your feet back to the ground on an exhale.

Variations to Extend the Pose

- If you have good balance, you can release your hands from the chair and extend them forward, parallel to the ground, alongside your legs.

Cautions and Modifications

If sitting on the chair is uncomfortable, you can use a cushion or folded blanket for additional padding and support under your sit bones. Pregnant women should avoid deep core engagement and can modify the pose with shallower lifts of the legs or focus on engaging the pelvic floor muscles without lifting the legs.

Seated Eagle Arms Pose

The Seated Eagle Arms Pose is designed to enhance balance, focus, and flexibility. It primarily targets the shoulders, upper back, and hips. The intention is to create a sense of stability while improving posture and concentration. Stretches and strengthens the shoulders, enhancing mobility.

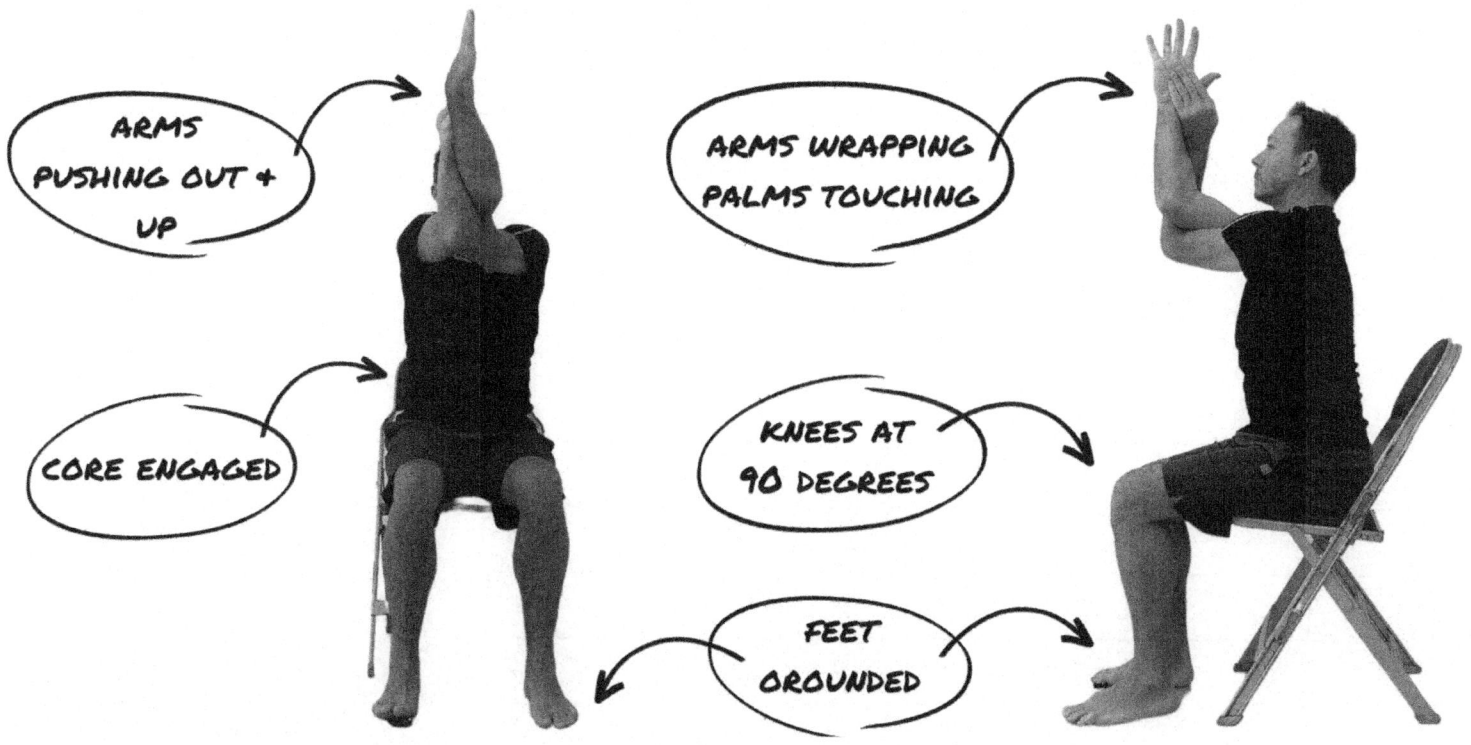

Steps to Achieve the Pose

- Sit in Easy Seating Pose
- Keep your spine straight, shoulders relaxed, and hands resting on your thighs.
- As you exhale, bring your elbow up to shoulder height and, forearms vertical.
- Cross your right arm under your left arm at the elbow joint, bringing the palms of your hands together. If this is too intense, hug yourself by placing your hands on opposite shoulders.
- Hold the pose for 20-30 seconds, breathing deeply and maintaining your balance.
- Release the arms and legs, returning to the starting position.
- Repeat on the other side, crossing your left arm under your right arm.

Variations to Extend the Pose

- To deepen the stretch, try to lift your elbows slightly higher while keeping your shoulders away from your ears.
- For a seated eagle twist, after coming into the eagle arms, gently twist to the right, then to the left, deepening the stretch in your upper back.

Cautions and Modifications

If bringing the palms together is challenging, use a strap or a cloth to hold onto, allowing your hands to be at a comfortable distance apart.

Notes

Lying Poses

Corpse Pose

Corpse Pose (Savasana), is a relaxation and meditative posture practiced at the end of a yoga session. The intention is to achieve a state of conscious relaxation, allowing the body to rest deeply while the mind remains alert and aware.

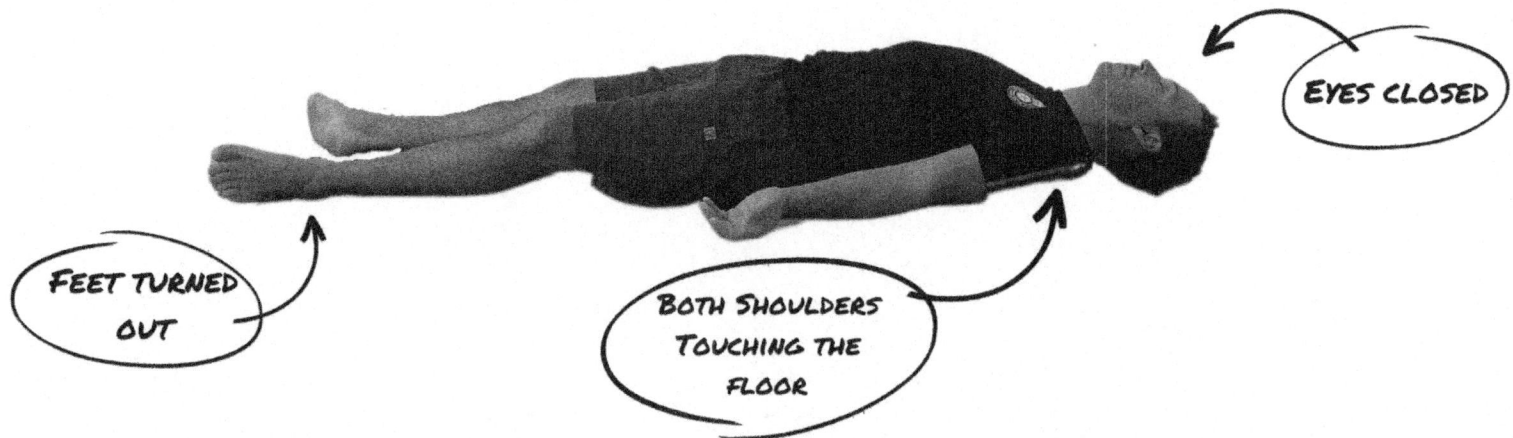

Steps to Achieve the Pose

- Lie on your back with your legs extended straight and arms resting alongside your body, palms facing up, allowing your feet to naturally fall open. Close your eyes gently.
- Close your eyes and take a few deep breaths, letting go of any tension with each exhale.
- Bring your awareness to different parts of your body, starting from your toes up to your head. As you focus on each body part, consciously release any tension you might be holding.
- Let go of controlling your breath. Allow your breathing to become natural and effortless.
- Relax your facial muscles, jaw, and tongue. Soften your shoulders and let your arms rest naturally, surrender your body entirely, feeling the support beneath you.
- Clear your mind of any thoughts. If your mind starts to wander, gently bring your focus back to your breath or a specific mantra or affirmation.
- Remain in Savasana for 5 to 10 minutes, depending on your preference and time availability.

Variations to Extend the Pose

- Body Scan: During Savasana, perform a mental body scan. Focus on each body part, sending it love and relaxation. Imagine each part becoming heavy and sinking down.
- Guided Visualisation: Listen to a guided meditation or visualisation to deepen your relaxation.
- Breath Awareness: Concentrate on the natural rhythm of your breath. Feel the rise and fall of your abdomen and chest with each breath.

Cautions and Modifications

If you have lower back issues, consider placing a small cushion or rolled-up towel under your knees to reduce the strain on your lower back. If you have neck discomfort, place a small cushion or folded towel under your neck for support. To enhance relaxation, you can place a light eye pillow over your eyes to block out light and promote a sense of darkness and inner focus.

Banana Pose

Banana Pose, (Bananasana), is a relaxing and gentle yoga stretch that aims to release tension in the spine and improve flexibility. The pose stretches the sides of the torso, promoting elongation of the intercostal muscles and improved breathing capacity.

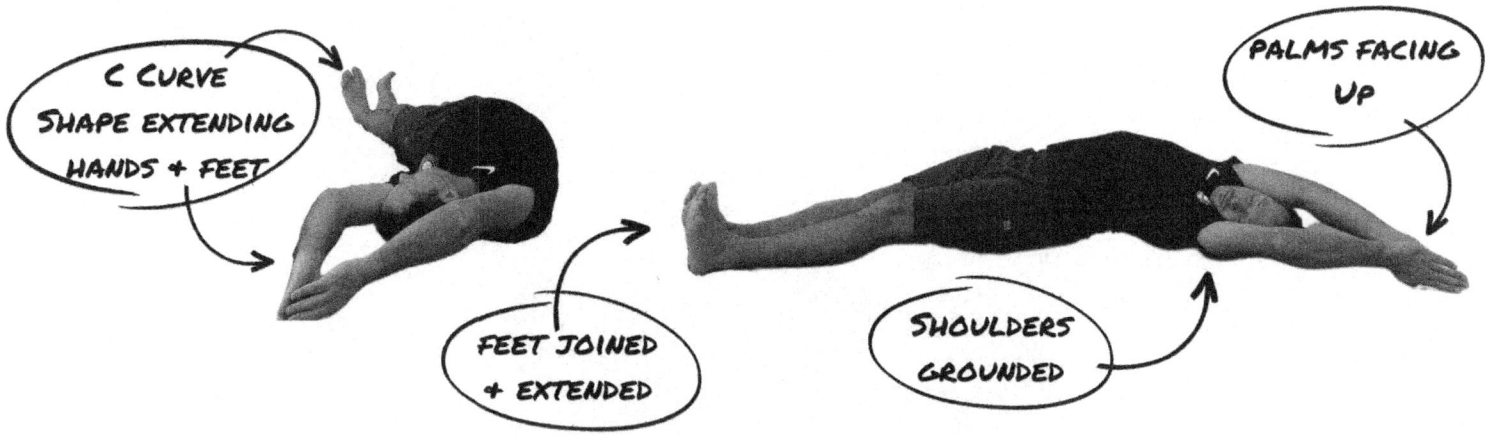

Steps to Achieve the Pose

- Begin by lying on your back in Corpse Pose.
- Place your arms overhead, clasping your hands together. Keep your palms facing upwards and join your feet together.
- Ensure your head and neck are in a neutral position, and your spine is in a straight line.
- Exhale and start to arch your body bringing your hands and feet to the right side, creating a gentle C-curve shape with your body. Keep both shoulders grounded.
- Inhale and come back to the centre, then exhale and arch your body to the left, mirroring the stretch on the opposite side.

Variations to Extend the Pose

- Legs Crossed: For a deeper stretch, cross your right ankle over your left ankle and vice versa while practicing the pose. This intensifies the stretch along the sides of the body.

Cautions and Modifications

If you have back injuries or discomfort, practice this stretch with caution and keep the movements gentle. Avoid forcing your body into deep stretches. If you have neck issues, place a small, folded towel or cushion under your neck to provide support and maintain a neutral spine. If you experience discomfort in your lower back or hips, consider placing a folded blanket or cushion under your knees to reduce strain on the lower back.

Knees-to-Chest Pose

Knees-to-Chest Pose, (Apanasana), is a restorative yoga posture that focuses on grounding and releasing tension in the lower back, hips, and abdomen. Gently stretches and relaxes the lower back muscles, providing relief from discomfort or stiffness.

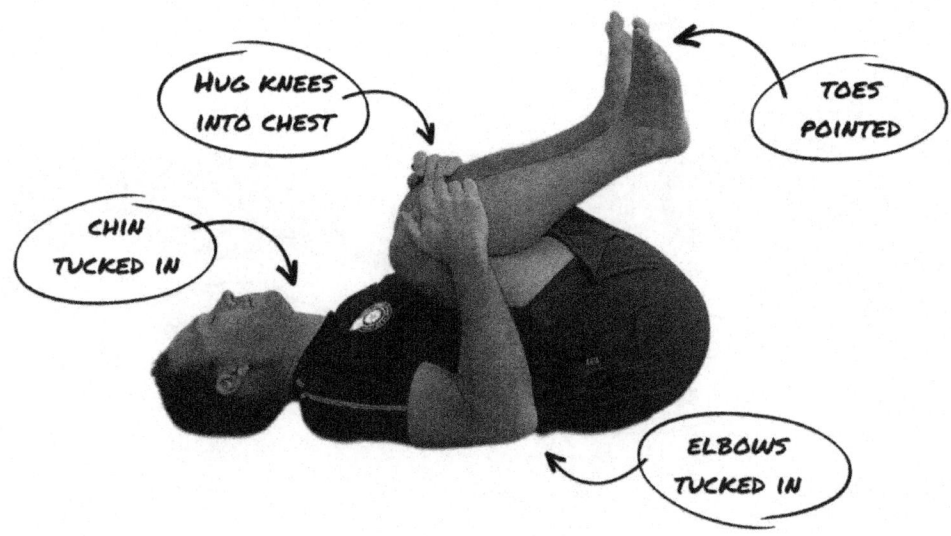

Steps to Achieve the Pose

- Lie on your back in a comfortable and relaxed position.
- Extend your legs straight or keep them slightly bent if it's more comfortable.
- Place your arms alongside your body with your palms facing down.
- On an exhale, bend your knees and bring them toward your chest.
- Hug your knees with your arms, holding your shins or clasping your hands around your knees. Keep your elbows close to your body. Relax your shoulders and neck.
- Let your lower back gently press downward. Keep your head and neck on the floor, or you can slightly lift your head, bringing your forehead toward your knees if it feels comfortable.
- Close your eyes and focus on your breath. Take slow, deep breaths, feeling your abdomen rise on each inhale and fall on each exhale.
- Hold the pose for several breaths, allowing your body to relax and soften with each breath.
- To release the pose, let go of your knees and extend your legs back to the starting position.

Variations to Extend the Pose

- Happy Baby Variation: From Knees-to-Chest Pose, you can move into Happy Baby Pose by grabbing the outer edges of your feet with your hands, bringing your knees toward your armpits.

Cautions and Modifications

If you have back injuries, practice this pose with caution and avoid pulling your knees too close to your chest. Keep the movements gentle and pain-free. Pregnant individuals can practice a modified version of this pose by keeping the legs wider apart to accommodate the belly. If you have neck issues, place a small, folded towel or cushion under your head to provide support and maintain a neutral neck position.

Legs Up the Wall Pose

Legs Up the Wall Pose, (Viparita Karani), is a restorative yoga posture that promotes relaxation, reduces stress, and provides gentle relief to tired legs. Elevating the legs above the heart promotes venous blood flow back to the heart, reducing swelling in the legs and ankles. Provides the benefits of an inversion without the strain on the neck and shoulders.

Steps to Achieve the Pose

- Begin by sitting sideways with your right side against the wall.
- Gently swing your legs up onto the wall as you lie down on your back. Turn so your sitting bones should be close to the wall, and your legs extended straight up.
- Adjust your position so that you are comfortably resting against the wall.
- Place your arms wherever you feel comfortable, palms facing down.
- Relax your head and neck, allowing your chin to slightly tuck toward your chest.
- Close your eyes and focus on your breath. Breathe deeply and slowly, relaxing completely.
- Hold the pose for 5 to 15 minutes, or longer if desired. Focus on deep, rhythmic breathing to enhance relaxation.

Variations to Extend the Pose

- Supported Legs Up the Wall: Place a folded blanket or bolster under your hips for added support and comfort. This variation reduces strain on the lower back and enhances relaxation.
- Wide-Legged Legs Up the Wall: Open your legs into a wide "V" shape, allowing gravity to gently stretch your inner thighs and groin.

Cautions and Modifications

Individuals with lower back injuries should place a folded blanket or cushion under their hips for additional support and reduce the duration of the pose if discomfort arises. Pregnant women can practice this pose with a cushion or bolster under their hips and avoid spreading their legs too wide.

Notes

Lying Twist Poses

Supine Spinal Twist Pose

Supine Spinal Twist Pose, (Supta Matsyendrasana), is a gentle yoga pose that focuses on stretching and releasing tension in the spine, shoulders, and hips. This twisting posture is intended to improve spinal mobility, alleviate lower back pain, and promote relaxation.

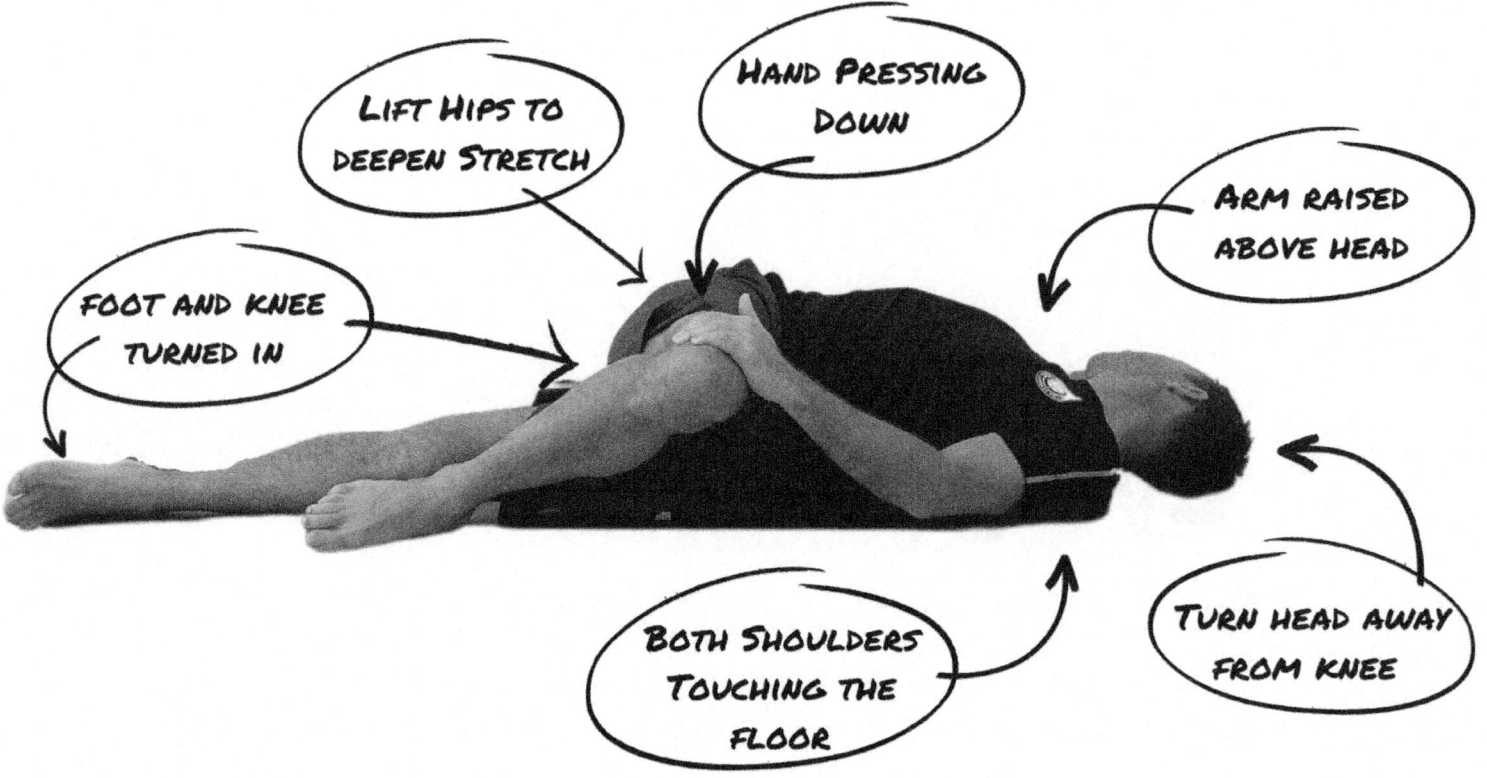

Steps to Achieve the Pose

- Begin by lying on your back, legs extended, placing your hands above your head.
- Keeping both shoulders grounded on an exhale, bend your right knee, place your left hand on your right knee and, twisting from the lower back, bring your right foot across your left knee.
- Turn your head to the left, looking in the opposite direction of your knees.
- Hold the twist for 30 seconds to 1 minute, breathing deeply and relaxing into the stretch.
- Inhale return to your knees and head to the centre.
- Exhale and repeat the twist on the other side.

Variations to Extend the Pose

- Both Legs Variation: Bending your left knee, tuck your right foot behind your left knee and twist.

Cautions and Modifications

Individuals with back injuries or conditions should approach this pose with caution. If you have a back injury, consider practicing this twist under the guidance of a yoga teacher. Should you experience discomfort in your knees, you can place a cushion or folded blanket between your knees for support. If you feel strain in your neck, you can place a small, folded towel or cushion under your head to support your neck during the twist.

Windscreen Wiper Pose

Windscreen Wiper Pose, (Supta Sucirandhrasana), is a supine yoga posture that offers a gentle stretch to the hips, inner thighs, and lower back. This pose is excellent for increasing flexibility in the hip joints and improving the range of motion in the legs.

Steps to Achieve the Pose

- Begin by lying on your back, legs extended, placing your hands out to your side in a T shape.
- Bend your knees and bring your feet flat on the floor.
- Inhale and on the exhale, lower your knees to the right side of your body while keeping both shoulders grounded. Feel a gentle stretch in your left hip and thigh. Hold the position for a few breaths, allowing your body to relax into the stretch.
- Inhale and bring your knees back to the centre, aligning them with your hips. Take a moment to centre yourself and relax.
- Exhale and lower your knees to the left side, keeping both shoulders rooted. Feel the stretch in your right hip and thigh. Breathe deeply, allowing the stretch to release tension in the muscles.
- Continue this gentle side-to-side movement, resembling the motion of windshield wipers, for several rounds of breath. Move slowly and mindfully, syncing your breath with the movement.

Variations to Extend the Pose

- Overlapping Leg Variation: For a deeper stretch, you can take the foot of the leg with the knee closest to the floor and place it on the outside of your other knee to act as a lever.

Cautions and Modifications

Approach this pose with caution if you have a back injury. If you have any recent or chronic hip or knee injury, approach this pose with caution. If you experience strain in your neck, consider placing a small, folded towel or cushion under your head to support your neck during the twist. Pregnant individuals should modify the pose by keeping the twist gentle and avoiding deep twists.

NOTES

Lying Core Body Poses

Boat Pose

Boat Pose, (Navasana), is a core-strengthening yoga posture that engages the abdominal muscles and improves balance. Boat Pose targets the core muscles, including the abdomen, hip flexors, and lower back, providing a robust core workout.

Steps to Achieve the Pose

- Sit with your back straight and your legs extended straight.
- Place your hands beside your hips, fingers pointing toward your feet.
- Engage your core muscles and lean back slightly, balancing on your sit bones.
- Inhale, lift your legs off the floor, bringing them to a 45-degree angle from the ground.
- Simultaneously, reach out and straighten your arms, parallel to the ground, palms facing each other.
- Keep your back straight, chest lifted, and shoulder blades relaxed.
- Hold the pose, breathing deeply, and maintaining a strong core engagement.
- To release the pose, lower your legs and arms, relaxing the pose.

Variations to Extend the Pose

- Extended Boat Pose: While in the pose, slowly lower and raise your upper body and legs closer without touching the floor, intensifying the workout.

Cautions and Modifications

Individuals with lower back problems can modify by keeping their hands behind their hips for support and bending their knees slightly. **If** you experience neck strain, keep your gaze forward instead of looking up. Beginners can bend their knees and hold the back of their thighs for added support while gradually building strength.

Lying Lower Body Poses

Reclining Bound Angle Pose

Reclining Bound Angle Pose, also known as Butterfly Pose, (Baddha Konasana), is a hip-opening yoga posture that encourages flexibility in the hips and inner thighs. It is practiced to improve posture, stimulate abdominal organs, and relieve mild depression and fatigue. Stretches and opens the hips, groin, and inner thighs, improving flexibility.

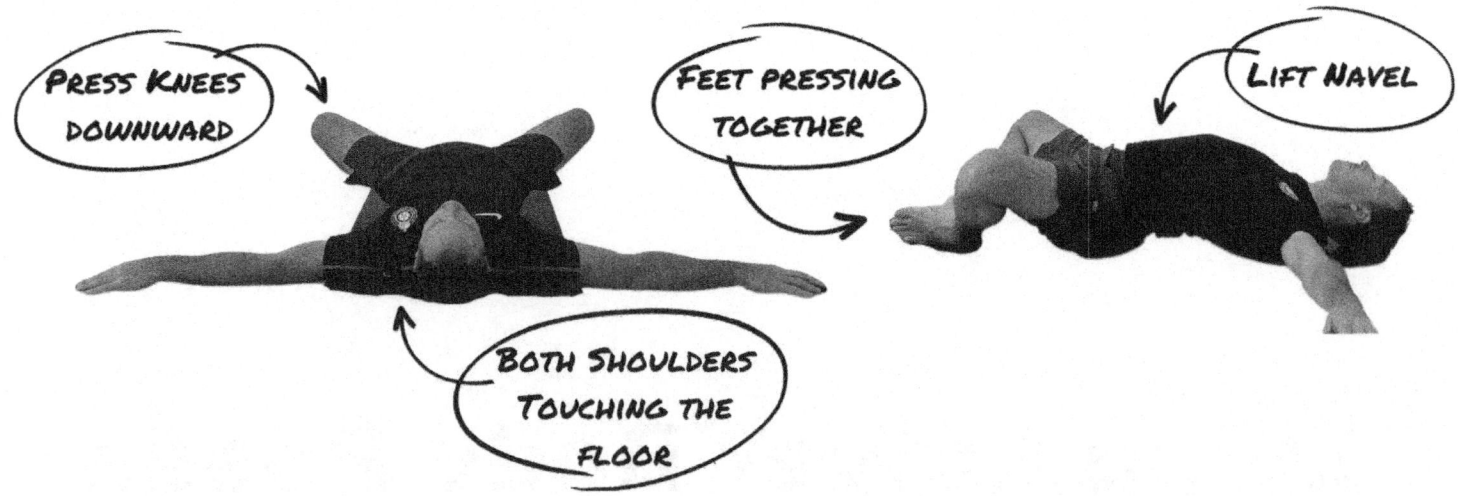

Steps to Achieve the Pose

- Begin by lying down in Corpse Pose, bend your knees and bring the soles of your feet together, allowing your knees to drop out to the sides.
- Hold your feet with your hands, bringing your heels as close to your pelvis as comfortable.
- Place hands above your head, out to the side or in surrender to keep shoulders in contact with the ground.
- Inhale and lengthen your spine.
- Exhale and gently press your knees downwards, feeling a stretch in your inner thighs and groin. Support your knees with cushions or bolsters to prevent strain on your inner thighs.
- Keep your spine straight and your chest lifted. Avoid rounding your back.
- Hold the pose for 30 seconds to a few minutes, breathing deeply and relaxing into the stretch.

Variations to Extend the Pose

- Seated Bound Angle Pose: Sit in Easy Seating Pose. Bring your feet together, allowing your knees to fall to the sides. Hold your feet and press down with your knees.
- Forward Fold Bound Angle Pose: While in Seated Bound Angle Pose, inhale deeply, then exhale as you hinge at your hips and lower your torso toward your feet. Hold your feet or rest your hands in front of you. This variation intensifies the stretch in your hips and lower back.

Cautions and Modifications

If you have knee or groin injuries, avoid pressing your knees too far down. Use cushions or rolled towels under your knees for support. Individuals with lower back injuries should sit on a folded blanket or cushion to elevate the hips and reduce strain on the lumbar spine. Pregnant women should practice this pose with support under their knees to avoid overstretching the pelvic area.

Happy Baby Pose

Happy Baby Pose, (Ananda Balasana), is practiced to release tension in the lower back, hips, and hamstrings. The gentle rocking motion of the pose massages the lower back, relieving discomfort, and tension. This pose offers a mild stretch to the hamstrings, enhancing their flexibility and provides a gentle release for the inner thigh muscles, promoting suppleness.

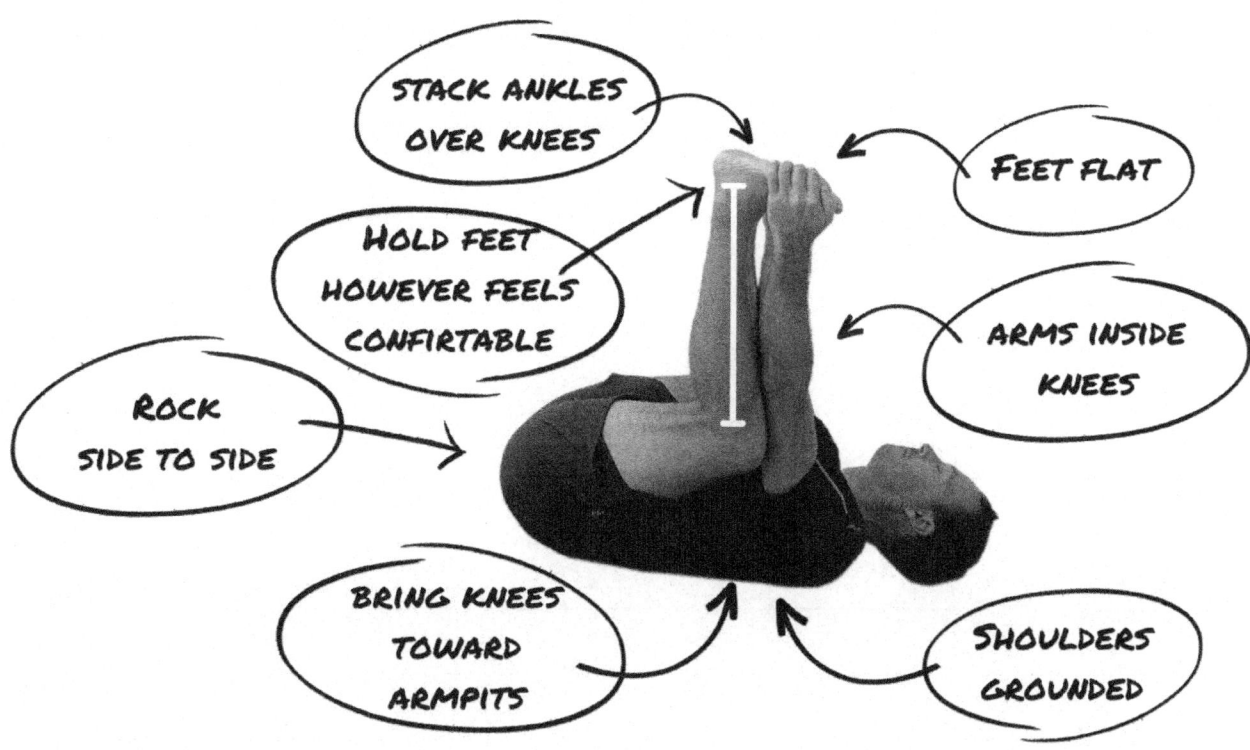

Steps to Achieve the Pose

- Lie on your back, exhale, and bend your knees into your belly.
- Inhale, hold the inside, outside, or big toes of your flat feet. Keep your arms on the inside of your knees.
- Open your knees wider than your torso and bring them toward your armpits. Flex your feet and stack your ankles directly above your knees.
- Ensure your ankles are aligned with your knees and your shins are perpendicular.
- Gently rock from side to side, massaging your lower back.
- Hold the pose for several breaths, allowing your body to relax and soften into the stretch.

Variations to Extend the Pose

- Happy Baby with Straps: If reaching your feet is challenging, use yoga straps looped around your feet, holding onto the ends for the stretch.

Cautions and Modifications

If you experience discomfort in your knees, place cushions or folded blankets under them for support. Pregnant individuals can modify by practicing a milder version of the pose, keeping the movements gentle and within a comfortable range of motion.

NOTES

Lying Back Bend Poses

Sphinx Pose

Sphinx Pose, (Salamba Bhujangasana), is a gentle backbend that aims to open the chest and stretch the front of the torso. It helps improve posture, strengthen the spine, and relieve mild backaches. This pose is often practiced to counteract the forward slouching that occurs from prolonged sitting.

Steps to Achieve the Pose

- Begin by lying on your stomach on a comfortable surface, with your legs extended straight, slightly wider than your hips, and your toes pointing back.
- Place your elbows directly under your shoulders, keeping your forearms parallel to each other, palms down. Press the tops of your feet down, engaging your leg muscles.
- On an inhale, press your forearms and palms down, lifting your chest and upper body. Your elbows should remain under your shoulders, and your pelvis should stay grounded.
- Keep your gaze forward, with your neck in line with your spine. Avoid crunching your neck or tilting your head too far back.
- Press your pubic bone gently downwards to support your lower back and engage your glutes and lower back muscles.
- Hold the pose for 20-30 seconds, breathing deeply and maintaining a comfortable stretch.

Variations to Extend the Pose

- Sphinx with Leg Lifts: For an added challenge, you can lift one leg at a time while maintaining the Sphinx position, engaging your glutes, and strengthening your lower back muscles.

Cautions and Modifications

If you have lower back issues, approach this pose with caution. Keep the backbend gentle and avoid straining your lower back. If you feel strain in your neck, keep your gaze forward and avoid tilting your head too far back. Pregnant individuals should avoid deep backbends. A modified, gentle Sphinx Pose with minimal lift can be practiced with proper support.

Upward Facing Dog Pose

Upward Facing Dog Pose, (Urdhva Mukha Svanasana), is a rejuvenating backbend that strengthens the spine, stretches the chest and lungs, and improves posture. Helps in correcting rounded shoulders and slouching by opening the chest and shoulders.

Steps to Achieve the Pose

- Lie on your stomach with your legs extended straight, hip-width apart, tops of your feet flat down.
- Place your palms beside your chest, fingers pointing forward and elbows bent at 90 degrees.
- Inhale as you press your palms down, straightening your arms and lifting your chest and upper body up.
- Engage your thigh muscles and press the tops of your feet firmly down, so your thighs lift.
- Roll your shoulders back and down, opening your chest forward. Keep your neck in a neutral position, looking straight ahead or slightly upward.
- Hold the pose for a few breaths, continuing to lift your chest and keeping your shoulders relaxed.
- Exhale as you gently lower your upper body back down.

Variations to Extend the Pose

- Deepen the Backbend: If you're comfortable, you can straighten your arms further, lifting your chest higher and arching your back more deeply.

Cautions and Modifications

People with back injuries should be cautious and avoid over-arching the spine. Keep the movement gentle and within a pain-free range. If you have wrist issues, you can practice a modified version by placing your forearms on the ground instead of straightening your arms. Pregnant individuals should practice with caution, avoiding excessive pressure on the abdomen.

Locust Pose

Locust Pose, (Shalabhasana), is a backbend that strengthens the entire back, including the lower, middle, and upper back muscles. This pose aims to improve posture, enhance spinal flexibility, and tone the buttocks and legs. It is often practiced to alleviate mild sciatica.

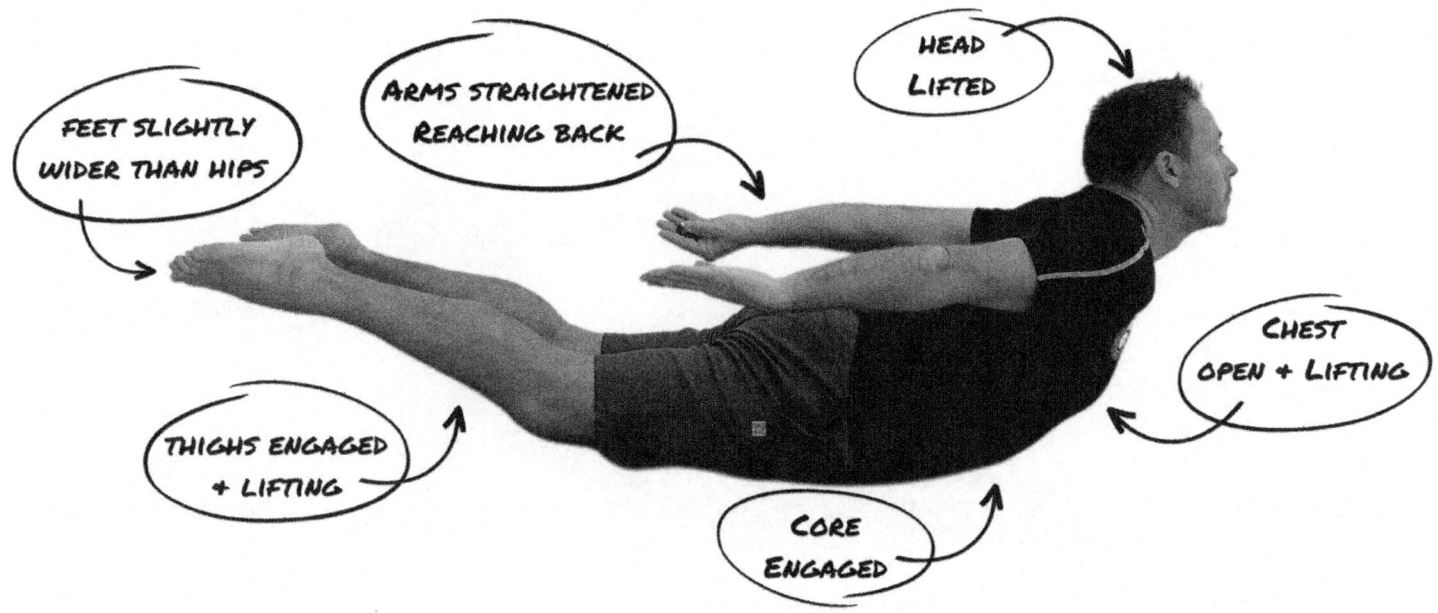

Steps to Achieve the Pose

- Lie on your stomach, feet wider than your hips and arms alongside your body, palms up.
- Rest your forehead on the ground, ensuring your neck is in a neutral position.
- Inhale as you lift your head, chest, arms, and legs off the ground. Engage your buttocks and back muscles.
- Keep your gaze level to maintain the natural curve in your neck. Avoid straining your neck by looking too high.
- Hold the pose for a few breaths. Lift your legs/chest higher with each inhale.
- Exhale as you gently release the pose, lowering your head, chest, arms, and legs back down.

Variations to Extend the Pose

- One-Leg Locust: Lift one leg at a time while keeping the other leg down. Alternate between legs to strengthen each leg individually.
- Arms Forward: Extend your arms forward alongside your ears while lifting in Locust Pose. This variation intensifies the backbend and strengthens the arms.

Cautions and Modifications

Individuals with back injuries should approach this pose with caution or avoid it altogether. Keep your neck in a neutral position and avoid lifting your head too high. If you experience neck strain, lower your head slightly. Pregnant individuals should modify this pose by lifting only their upper body while keeping the lower body anchored. Always consult a healthcare provider before practicing any yoga poses during pregnancy.

Cobra Pose

Cobra Pose, (Bhujangasana), aims to gently strengthen the back muscles, increase spinal flexibility, and open the chest. This pose intends to improve posture, relieving mild backaches by strengthening the lower and upper back muscles, promoting a healthy spine.

Steps to Achieve the Pose

- Lie face down, your legs extended, and the tops of your feet grounded, knees hip-width apart.
- Place your palms flat next to your shoulders, fingers spread, elbows close to your body.
- Inhale deeply, pressing down through your palms, and slowly lift your head, chest, and upper abdomen lifted. Use the strength of your back muscles to lift, not your arms, keep elbows bent.
- Keep your gaze forward or slightly upward, ensuring your neck is in a comfortable position, and squeeze your shoulders together to open your chest.
- Continue to press the tops of your feet down to maintain the connection with the ground.
- Engage your glutes and lower back muscles to support your lower spine.
- Breathe deeply and hold the pose for a few breaths, lengthening your spine with each inhalation and gently deepening the stretch with each exhalation.
- To release the pose, exhale and slowly lower your chest and head back down.

Variations to Extend the Pose

- Cobra with Hands Lifted: Instead of placing your palms flat, lift your palms a few inches off the ground, engaging your back muscles more intensely.

Cautions and Modifications

If you have a back injury or discomfort, avoid this pose, or practice it under the guidance of a yoga teacher to ensure proper alignment. Pregnant individuals should avoid deep backbends like Cobra, instead, they can practice the gentler Sphinx version.

Bridge Pose

Bridge Pose, (Setu Bandhasana), is aimed at gently energising the body and improving flexibility. It helps in strengthening the lower back, toning the legs, and opening the chest. Engaging and toning the muscles in the legs, including thighs and glutes.

Steps to Achieve the Pose

- Lie on your back with your knees bent and feet flat a hip-width apart.
- Place your arms alongside your body, palms facing down.
- Pull your shoulders together.
- Inhale and press your feet down, lifting your hips towards the ceiling and joining your hands together which will support your shoulders.
- Keep your knees parallel to each other and engage your glutes and core muscles.
- Lift your chest toward your chin, opening your throat and chest.
- Hold the pose for 20-30 seconds, breathing deeply and steadily.
- Exhale and gently release your hands, rolling your spine back down.

Variations to Extend the Pose

- To intensify the stretch, try walking your shoulders closer together, deepening the arch in your back.
- For a more restorative version, place a cushion or a folded blanket under your sacrum for support, allowing your hips to be slightly elevated.

Cautions and Modifications

Avoid over-arching your back, especially if you have lower back issues. Keep the natural curve of your spine. If your neck feels strained, keep your head grounded without lifting it. For additional back support, consider placing a bolster or a rolled-up blanket under your knees.

Developing Toothbrush Yoga Further — The Breath as Life Force

In the heart of Yoga itself lies the ancient art of Pranayama — the conscious control of breath, connecting the body, mind, and spirit in a harmonious dance of life force energy.

In Sanskrit, "Prana" means life force, and "Yama" means control, signifying the conscious regulation of breath to enhance physical, mental, and spiritual well-being.

Within the gentle cadence of inhales and exhales, Pranayama becomes a transformative practice, that can be intricately woven into the fabric of Toothbrush Yoga. Incorporating Pranayama into the Toothbrush Yoga framework, whether standalone or integral to the habitual practice offers a plethora of benefits that extend beyond the physical body, nurturing holistic well-being and enhancing the quality of life.

Pranayama balances the vital energies within your body — Prana, the upward-moving energy, and Apana, the downward-moving energy. Through specific breath control, you harmonise these energies, fostering equilibrium, stability, and a deep sense of inner peace.

Inhale the future, exhale the past. Yoga is the art of finding balance in the present moment.

Unknown

Benefits of Pranayama

- **Stress reduction** — Pranayama techniques promote relaxation by calming the nervous system, reducing stress, and alleviating anxiety and tension.
- **Enhanced mental clarity** — regular Pranayama clears the mind, improves focus, and boosts mental clarity, aiding in better decision-making and problem-solving.
- **Balanced energy** — Pranayama balances the flow of life energy (Prana) within the body, ensuring equilibrium and vitality.
- **Mindfulness** — Pranayama serves as a gateway to mindfulness, teaching practitioners to be present, enhancing self-awareness, and deepening the mind-body connection.
- **Better sleep** — Pranayama techniques, especially those focused on calming breath, promote relaxation, leading to improved sleep quality and duration.

Through conscious breathing, you unlock the gateway to mindfulness, balance, and holistic well-being. As you embrace the subtleties of your breath, you embark on a transformative journey, not only within the confines of Toothbrush Yoga but in every breath, in every moment, enriching your life with the essence of Pranayama.

How to Practice Pranayama

The following Pranayama techniques offer various benefits and can be practiced individually or incorporated into your yoga or meditation routines. As you engage in deep, rhythmic breathing, your body releases tension, and your mind finds tranquillity. With every inhale and exhale, you draw your focus inward, quieting the chatter of the mind. This heightened mindfulness not only enriches your yoga practice but permeates your daily life, infusing each moment with profound awareness.

- **Chest breathing** — chest breathing is where the chest expands during inhalation and contracts during exhalation. Inhale slowly through the nose and notice how your chest expands. Exhale gently through the nose, allowing your chest to contract. Focus on the rise and fall of your chest with each breath and the sensation of the breath through your body.
- **Belly breathing** — also known as diaphragmatic breathing, involves breathing deeply into the abdomen, allowing the diaphragm to fully expand. Inhale slowly through the nose, allowing your abdomen to expand outward. Exhale gently, letting your abdomen contract. Focus on the movement of your belly with each breath.
- **Ujjayi breath** — or victorious breath, involves breathing with a slight constriction at the back of your throat, creating a soft ocean-like sound. Inhale and exhale slowly through your nose, constricting the back of your throat slightly to create a subtle hissing sound. Focus on the sound and rhythm of your breath.
- **Nadi Shodhana/alternate nostril breathing** — balances the energy channels in the body by alternating the breath between nostrils. Use your thumb to close one nostril while inhaling through the other. Close the other nostril with your ring finger, and exhale through the first nostril. Then, reverse the process. This completes one cycle.
- **Bumblebee breath** — also called Bhramari Pranayama, it involves producing a humming sound during exhalation, calming the mind. Close your ears with your thumbs, place your index fingers on your forehead, and rest the remaining fingers on your closed eyes. Inhale deeply and exhale, making a humming sound like a bee. Repeat several times.
- **Sama Vritti (equal breathing)** — focuses on equalising the duration of inhalation and exhalation, promoting balance and relaxation. Inhale for a specific count (e.g. four seconds), then exhale for the same count. Maintain a consistent rhythm, gradually increasing the duration as your breath control improves.

APPENDIX

Notes

I have provided a list of references, and citations for the chapters within the book. Due to the nature of the web, these references may be moved and consequently, they may need to be updated. Furthermore, there may be errors or omissions within this book, through no intention, if you are aware of any incorrect information, be they attribution, credit where it is due, references, URLs, yoga poses, etc, please email me at rob.hales2@gmail.com so I can address them in future versions.

Introducing Toothbrush Yoga — Tiny Habits, Transformational Results

The New Rules of Stretching

https://tinyurl.com/Timesstretching

2016 Yoga in America Study Conducted by Yoga Journal and Yoga Alliance Reveals Growth and Benefits of the Practice

https://tinyurl.com/YA2016Study

My Path to Becoming a Toothbrush Yogi

Making and breaking habits

https://tinyurl.com/21-DayMyth

How are Habits Formed: Modelling Habit Formation in the Real World

https://tinyurl.com/RealWorldHabits

The Resolution Solution: Longitudinal Examination of New Year's Change Attempts

https://tinyurl.com/NY-Resolutions

Self-regulatory Goal Motivational Sustained New Year Resolution Pursuit and Mental Wellbeing. International Journal of Environmental Research and Public Health

https://tinyurl.com/NY-Resolutions2

Chapter 2: The Hidden Forces — Decoding the Mechanisms of Habits

Making and breaking habits — McGovern Institute

https://tinyurl.com/Mk-BkHabits

Harnessing the Power of Habits — The Habit Lab within the University of Southern California

https://tinyurl.com/HabitLab

Habit Loop: Charles Duhigg, The Power of Habit: Why We Do What We Do in Life and Business

Cue, Routine, Reward: Charles Duhigg, The Power of Habit: Why We Do What We Do in Life and Business

Cue, Craving Routine, Reward: James Clear, Atomic Habits: An Easy & Proven Way to Build Good Habits & Break Bad Ones

Chapter 3: Hijacking the Habit Flow

Habit Recipe: BJ Fogg Tiny Habits: The Small Changes that Change Everything

Habit Stacking: James Clear, Atomic Habits: An Easy & Proven Way to Build Good Habits & Break Bad Ones

The Importance of Creating Habits and Routine

https://tinyurl.com/HabitRoutines

How are habits formed: Modelling Habit Formation in the Real World

https://tinyurl.com/ModellingHabits

Chapter 4: My Toothbrush Yoga Framework — Morning Ritual

The Times — The New Rules of Stretching

https://tinyurl.com/Timesstretching

British Journal of Sports Medicine — Successful 10-Second One-Legged Stance Performance Predicts Survival in Middle-aged and Older Individuals

https://tinyurl.com/10secbalance

Chapter 5: Toothbrush Yoga at Work/Study

ONS — Average actual weekly hours of work for full-time workers (seasonally adjusted)

https://tinyurl.com/ONSFTE

Chapter 6: Toothbrush Yoga in Everyday Tasks

The physiological effects of slow breathing in the healthy human

https://tinyurl.com/Slow-Breathing

Chapter 8: Your Toothbrush Yoga Framework

Mindset Theory of Action Phases

https://tinyurl.com/Mindset-Theory

How are Habits Formed: Modelling Habit Formation in the Real World

https://tinyurl.com/RealWorldHabits

Combining Motivational and Volitional Interventions to Promote Exercise Participation: Protection Motivation Theory and Implementation Intentions

https://tinyurl.com/ExcerMotivation

The Impact of Commitment, Accountability, and Written Goals on Goal Achievement

https://tinyurl.com/WrittenGoals

New Developments in Goal Setting and Task Performance

https://tinyurl.com/Goal-Setting-Task

Chapter 10: Counting the Streak — The Power of Habit-Tracking Apps

Habit Tracker

https://apps.apple.com/us/app/habit-tracker/id1438388363

Habit Tracker + Daily Planner

https://apps.apple.com/gb/app/habit-tracker-daily-planner/id1661598291

Habit Kit

https://apps.apple.com/gb/app/habit-tracker-habitkit/id6443918070

Done

https://apps.apple.com/gb/app/done-a-simple-habit-tracker/id1103961876

Free Bonus Content

To unlock exclusive bonus content, I invite you to join the Toothbrush Yoga newsletter community. By signing up at https://tinyurl.com/ToothbrushYogaBonusContent, you'll gain access to a wealth of free Toothbrush Yoga Journal Templates, that can be used as part of your Toothbrush Yoga Intention Mapping, Goal Setting/Tracking and Journaling:

- A Line-A-Day Journal
- Habit Flow Map
- Intention Mapping Flow Chart
- Practice Calculation
- Daily Journal
- Daily Progress
- Weekly Progress
- Weekly Habit Trackers
- Monthly Habit Trackers
- Goal Tracker
- Short-term Goal Tracker
- Long-term Goal Tracker
- 30 Day Challenges

Once you've signed up, an email will be sent directly to your inbox containing a special link that will grant you entry to the bonus content. This valuable resource includes additional yoga sequences, guided meditations, expert tips, and much more, all carefully curated to elevate your practice and bring further transformation to your daily routine.

Don't miss out on this opportunity to deepen your connection with Toothbrush Yoga and receive valuable tools to support your wellness journey. Join the newsletter community today and unlock the door to a world of complimentary content that will empower and inspire you along your yoga path.

English/Sanskrit Pose Names

The poses mentioned in this book may have various names depending on the yoga traditions and instructors. This list includes the English names I have used, their Sanskrit equivalents, and alternative English names, all referring to the identical pose.

Standing Poses

Mountain Pose/Tadasana

Forward Fold Pose/Uttanasana - Standing Forward Bend, Standing Forward Fold, Standing Jackknife Pose, Standing Hands-to-Feet Pose

Half Lift Pose/Ardha Uttanasana - Half Standing Forward Fold, Half Forward Fold, Half Forward Bend, Flat Back Pose, Chest Lift Pose

Chair Pose/Utkatasana - Fierce Pose, Powerful Pose, Lightning Bolt Pose, Awkward Pose, Thunderbolt Pose, Wild Pose, Extended Squat Pose, Toe Squat Pose

Standing Balance Poses

Tree Pose/Vrikshasana - Standing Tree Pose, Tree Balancing Pose, Tree Position, Tree Asana

Vrksasana

Eagle Pose/Garudasana - Standing Eagle Pose, Wrapped Eagle Pose, Eagle Pose Twist

Dancer Pose/Natarajasana - Lord of the Dance Pose, King Dancer Pose, Dancing Shiva Pose, Dancing Pose

Standing Sequence Poses

Warrior 1 Pose/Virabhadrasana I - Powerful Warrior Pose, High Lunge Pose, Crescent Pose, Brave Pose

Warrior 2 Pose/Virabhadrasana II - Strong Warrior Pose, Side Warrior Pose, Open-Armed Warrior Pose, Extended Warrior Pose

Reverse Warrior Pose/Viparita Virabhadrasana - Reverse Warrior Stretch, Reversed Warrior Pose, Flipped Warrior Pose

Warrior 3 Pose/Virabhadrasana III - Airplane Pose, Flying Warrior Pose, Balancing Warrior Pose, Extended Leg Warrior Pose

Extended Side Angle Pose/Utthita Parsvakonasana - Extended Lateral Angle Pose, Extended Side Stretch Pose, Elongated Flank Pose

Triangle Pose/Utthita Trikonasana - Extended Triangle Stretch, Extended Triangle Asana, Extended Three-Angle Pose

Low Lunge Pose/Anjaneyasana - Kneeling Lunge Pose

Crescent Lunge Pose/Anjaneyasana - Moon Pose, High Runner's Lunge

Kneeling Poses

Tabletop Pose/Bharmanasana - Table Pose, All-Fours Pose, Quadruped Pose, Hands and Knees Pose, Neutral Spine Pose

Child's Pose/Balasana - Resting Pose, Extended Child's Pose, Embryo Pose, Hare Pose

Cat/Cow Pose/Marjaryasana/Bitilasana - Spinal Warm-up Pose

Frog Pose/Mandukasana - Sitting Frog Pose

Camel Pose/Ustrasana - Back Bend Pose, Deep Arch Pose

Downward Dog Pose/Adho Mukha Svanasana - Downward Facing Dog Pose, Down Dog Pose

Plank Pose/Phalakasana - High Plank Pose, Straight Arm Plank, Staff Pose

Pigeon Pose/Eka Pada Rajakapotasana - One-Legged King Pigeon Pose, Sleeping Pigeon Pose, Half Pigeon Pose

Seated Poses

Easy Seating Pose/Sukhasana - Easy Pose, Comfortable Pose, Pleasant Pose, Simple Cross-Legged Pose, Classic Sitting Pose, Adequate Pose

Half Lotus Pose/Ardha Padmasana - Half Bound Lotus Pose, Modified Lotus Pose

Seated Side Bend Pose/Parsva Sukhasana - Seated Easy Side Twist, Side Seated Pose, Easy Side Pose

Seated Side Twist Pose/Parivrtta Sukhasana - Seated Twist Pose, Easy Seated Twist, Twisted Easy Pose, Seated Half Twist, Simple Twist Pose

Seated Cat/Cow Pose/Marjarasana/Bitilasana Variation

Seated Forward Bend Pose/Paschimottanasana Variation

Seated Pigeon Pose/Eka Pada Rajakapotasana Variation

Seated Boat Pose/Navasana Variation

Seated Eagle Arms Pose/Garudasana on a Chair Variation

Lying Poses

Corpse Pose/Savasana - Final Relaxation Pose, Deep Relaxation Pose, Relaxation Pose, Dead Body Pose

Banana Pose/Bananasana - Crescent Moon Pose, Swaying Palm Tree Pose, Curved Side Stretch Pose, Side Bend Pose, Half Moon Pose

Knees-to-Chest Pose/Apanasana - Wind-Relieving Pose, Reclined Knees-to-Chest Pose, Balancing Wind Pose, Hugging Knees Pose

Legs Up the Wall Pose/Viparita Karani - Inverted Lake Pose, Supported Shoulderstand Variation, Restorative Legs Up The Wall Pose, Rejuvenating Pose, Upside-Down Relaxation Pose

Lying Twist Poses

Supine Spinal Twist/Supta Matsyendrasana - Reclining Twist, Supine Lord of the Fishes Pose, Reclined Twist Pose, Twisted Lying Pose

Windscreen Wiper Pose/ Supta Sucirandhrasana – Windscreen Wiper Pose

Lying Core Body Poses

Boat Pose/Navasana - Full Boat Pose, Half Boat Pose, V-shape Pose

Lying Lower Body Poses

Reclining Bound Angle Pose/Baddha Konasana - Butterfly Pose, Cobbler's Pose, Butterfly Bound Pose, Clasped Angle Pose

Happy Baby Pose/Ananda Balasana - Blissful Baby Pose, Dead Bug Pose, Floating Baby Pose

Lying Back Bend Poses

Sphinx Pose/Salamba Bhujangasana - Supported Cobra Pose, Low Cobra Pose

Upward Facing Dog Pose/Urdhva Mukha Svanasana - Up Dog Pose, Upward Dog Pose, Raised Dog Pose, Upward-Facing Canine Pose

Locust Pose/Shalabhasana - Grasshopper Pose, Flying Locust Pose, Superman Pose

Cobra Pose/Bhujangasana - Serpent Pose, Snake Pose, Backbend Cobra Pose

Bridge Pose/Setu Bandhasana - Supported Bridge Pose, Half Wheel Pose, Half Bridge Pose

Acknowledgements

Upon arriving back from my travels around the World, I was waiting for the Universe to provide me with a path to my next purpose. Whilst waiting for that to turn up I decided to write this book! Maybe the absence of any else to do provided me with the creative spark and opportunity to invest the time to create Toothbrush Yoga. I am profoundly grateful for the energy that has propelled this project forward and for the harmony that permeates every page.

Writing a book is not a solitary endeavour, and this project wouldn't have come to fruition without the support, encouragement, and expertise of numerous individuals. I am profoundly grateful for the contributions of those who have guided, inspired, and stood by me throughout this process. I express my deepest gratitude to:

The American Language

The word practice or practise has two spellings in English, one for a noun and one for a verb. It became impossible for me to determine if a sentence such as "you can practice a modified version by placing your forearms on the ground" was in fact a verb or a noun. So with gratitude, I've stuck with the American spelling! Apologies to all English spellers out there, and particularly to Jessica Ward who tried to correct this so many times in her edits of this book!

That's why it's called a practice. We have to practice a practice if it is to be of value.

Peace Pilgrim

My Family

To Rachel and my girls, thank you for not laughing when I told you I was writing a book about yoga.

My Yoga Mentors

I extend my heartfelt thanks to my yoga mentors and teachers, whose wisdom and teachings have enlightened my path. Your guidance has been instrumental in shaping the content of this book and my personal yoga journey.

My Readers

To everyone who parted with their hard-earned money to buy this book and all the readers who have provided feedback, shared their experiences, and offered invaluable suggestions, thank you for being an essential part of this creative process. Your insights have enriched the narrative and added depth to the concepts explored in these pages.

The Research Community

I am indebted to the researchers, scholars, and experts in the fields of yoga, habit formation, and mindfulness. Your ground-breaking studies and findings have not only enlightened me but have also lent credibility to the content of this book.

My Editor and Proof-readers

A special thanks to my editor and proof-readers, whose meticulous attention to detail, constructive feedback, and editorial expertise transformed my words into a polished manuscript. Your dedication to enhancing the clarity and coherence of this book is deeply appreciated.

My Inspirations

To the authors, yogis, and thinkers whose works have inspired me, thank you for sharing your knowledge and insights with the world. Your contributions have influenced the direction of this book and broadened my understanding of yoga and mindful living.

To all of you, my heartfelt thanks. Your contributions, whether big or small, have made an indelible mark on this book, and for that, I am truly grateful.

With deepest appreciation,

Rob

About the Author

I'm Rob Hales, a man who has defied the conventional wisdom that you can't teach an old dog new tricks. In fact, I didn't just learn a new trick; I mastered the ancient art of yoga at the ripe age of 50!

Picture this, a man in his fifties, mid-life crisis in full swing, feeling the subtle yet undeniable signs of ageing creeping up on him. Recognising that his body needed some serious maintenance to keep up with the demands of time. Rather than do what any sensible person would do, I embarked on a quest, not to find the Fountain of Youth, but to uncover the Secrets of Yoga.

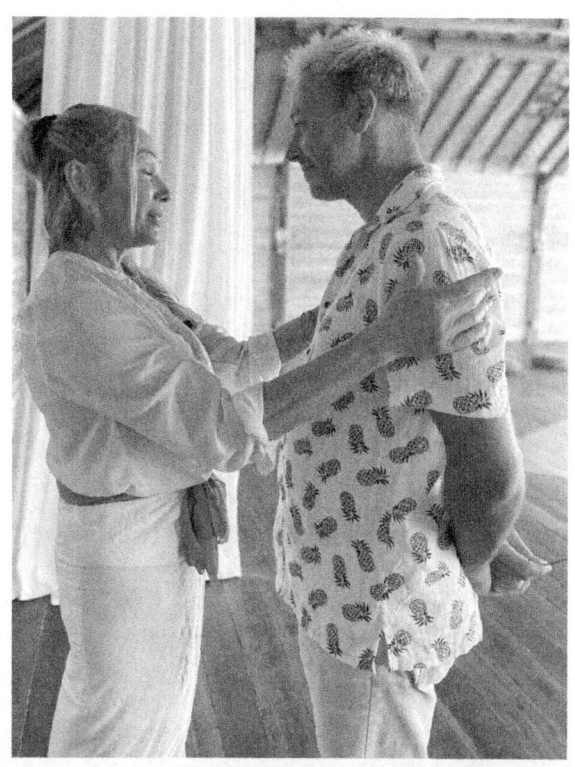

Now, here's where the story takes a delightful turn. Instead of attending a conventional yoga class in a serene studio with gentle instrumental music in the background, I decided to become a yoga teacher while gallivanting around a Balinese island! Bali, the land of lush greenery, serene beaches, and, apparently, yoga epiphanies.

It's fair to say that my journey to yoga mastery was sprinkled with moments of hilarity, humility, and a fair share of "I can't believe I'm doing this" thoughts. After all, why should the path to enlightenment be solemn when it can be a delightful, laughter-filled adventure?

Santosha

SANTOSHA 200 HOUR YOGA TEACHER TRAINING

In recognition of diligent practice and study

Rob Hales

has passed the necessary requirements and completed the full 200 hours of intensive study in the foundations and teaching practices of Yoga and is granted the license and title of Certified 200 Hour Yoga Teacher

Sunny Richards

23 May, 2023

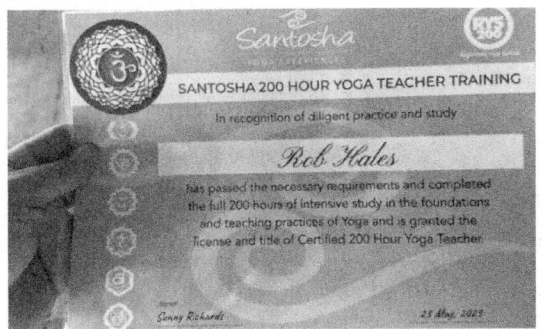

While exploring the enchanting landscapes of Southeast Asia, I stumbled upon James Clear's book, “Atomic Habits”. As I devoured the pages, I had a flash of inspiration that was as illuminating as the Balinese sunrises. I realised I could incorporate the concepts of habit stacking into my daily rituals, modifying my deeply ingrained habit flows to seamlessly incorporate yoga practice, without the need to attend formal yoga classes.

After immersing myself in yoga teacher training in Bali, I spent time attempting to strike a perfect yoga pose on the beaches only to be photobombed by a curious monkey or two, all while researching the fundamentals of behavioural science.

As you delve into the transformative wisdom of these pages, remember that they were crafted by a man who not only embraced yoga later in life but now starts every day bent double with a toothbrush and finishes with legs akimbo reading a book.

My hope for this book is that it will get you ready to bend and stretch your way to a healthier, happier you. I hope I can prove that it's never too late to embark on a journey of self-discovery, even if it involves yoga poses, monkeys, and a healthy dose of humour.

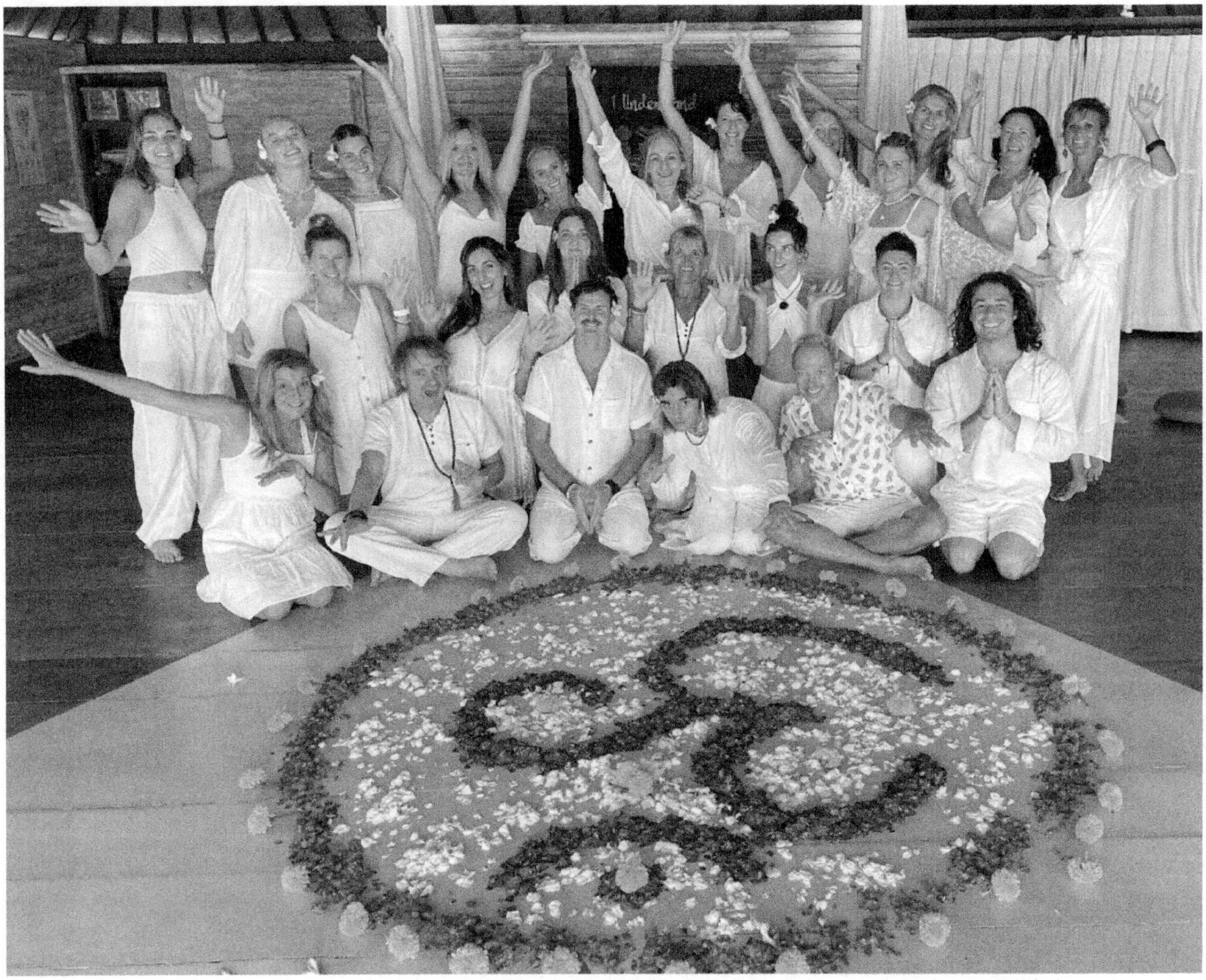

Printed in Great Britain
by Amazon